MW01136991

AUTHENTIC MANHOOD

This book can be optimized for group study.
A Leader's Guide is available for purchase -
scan QR code to access.

DAILY REFLECTIONS FOR MEN

AUTHENTIC MANHOOD

Book II
A MAN AND HIS STORY

Steve Snider

invite
PRESS
Plano, Texas

AUTHENTIC MANHOOD:
DAILY REFLECTIONS FOR MEN / BOOK II: A MAN AND HIS STORY
Copyright © 2025 by Steve Snider

All rights reserved.

This book is printed on acid-free, elemental chlorine-free paper.

ISBN: Paperback 978-1-963265-46-0. eBook 978-1-963265-47-7

Unless otherwise noted, Scripture quotations are from the ESV® Bible (The Holy Bible, English Standard Version®), © 2001 by Crossway, a publishing ministry of Good News Publishers. Used by permission. All rights reserved.

Scripture quotations marked NIV are taken from the Holy Bible, New International Version®, NIV® Copyright ©1973, 1978, 1984, 2011 by Biblica, Inc.™ Used by permission of Zondervan. All rights reserved worldwide.

Scripture quotations marked NKJV are taken from the New King James Version®. Copyright © 1982 by Thomas Nelson. Used by permission. All rights reserved.

24 25 26 27 28 29 30 31 32 33—10 9 8 7 6 5 4 3 2 1
MANUFACTURED in the UNITED STATES of AMERICA

Contents

A Man and His Story   xi

Day 1
Story   1

Day 2
Seeking Renewal in a Broken
World   5

Day 3
Finger Pointing   7

Day 4
When Life Hits You
in the Face   9

Day 5
Bigger Than Life   11

Day 6
The Influence of Mom   13

Day 7
Breaking Free from the "All-
Alone Wound"   15

Day 8
Taking the First Step Toward
Healing   17

Day 9
It's Complicated   19

Day 10
Walking the Tightrope   21

Day 11
Strength in Vulnerability   23

Day 12
Rooted in the Midst of Life's
Storms   25

Day 13
Seeing Beyond Your Blind
Spots   29

Day 14
Authenticity in the Face of
Loss   31

Day 15
The Art of Shaping Glass   33

Day 16
The Restless Soul   35

Day 17
Effects of a Mother Wound   37

Day 18
The Perfectionist's Journey
to Grace and Healing   41

Day 19
Being a Life-Giving Spirit   45

Day 20
Embracing the Dark Night
of the Soul   49

Day 21
The Great Paradox of Death
and Resurrection   51

Day 22
Inner Tool Chest   53

Day 23
What Every Son Needs
from Dad   55

Day 24
Unlocking Your Heart   59

Day 25
The Healing Power of a
Healthy Marriage   61

Day 26
Fixing Our Eyes on Jesus   63

Day 27
The Healing Power of
Honest Sharing   67

Day 28
My Emotional Hunger   69

Day 29
Breaking the Cycle
of Criticism   71

Contents

Day 30
Healthy Boundaries   73

Day 31
Listening to the Stories Our
Bodies Are Telling Us   75

Day 32
Rest and Restoration   79

Day 33
Seeing Your Story Clearly   81

Day 34
Facing the Tiger   83

Day 35
From Earthly Wounds to
Heavenly Healing   87

Day 36
Untangling the Apron
Strings   89

Day 37
The Healed Man   91

Day 38
Cultivating Connection
through Healing   95

Day 39
Surrendering the Flag   97

Day 40
Diffusing the Pressure
Within   99

Day 41
Growing into Your Own
Shoes   101

Day 42
Scars and Stories   103

Day 43
The Freedom of
Forgiveness   105

Day 44
Lifting the Manhole Cover   107

Day 45
Navigating the Journey with
Others   109

Day 46
Unhealthy Shame Hinders
Healing   111

Day 47
Breaking the Generational
Cycle of Pain   113

Day 48
Moving Forward in Grieving
and Grace   115

Day 49
Facing the Monsters Within 117

Day 50
The Shaping Power of a
Father's Words   119

Day 51
Pause and Reflect   121

Day 52
The Courage to Lean In   123

Day 53
The Heart Wound   125

Day 54
Nourishing Your Emotional
and Spiritual Health   127

Day 55
The River Within   129

Day 56
Intentional Time, Intentional
Talk   131

Day 57
From Observer to
Participant   133

Day 58
Stepping Out from Behind
the Screen   135

Day 59
Overcoming Anxiety and
Embracing Healing   137

Day 60
Embracing the Journey   139

*To my family, who, along with Christ,
is at the center of my story.*

A MAN AND HIS STORY

Your Past Experiences Are Shaping Who You Are Today

- Your personal story includes your memories, your interpretations of those memories, and how those memories shape your view of yourself. A lot of your story is formed during your childhood years, which has, and will continue, to influence every aspect of your life.

- Every man has wounds. Yes, you have wounds. As a human being, in addition to happy and joyful memories, you have experienced hurts, heartaches, failures, and losses that have left their marks on you in some way or another. Your wounds are part of your story.

- If you take steps to heal your inner wounds, your scars can serve as a vital source of wisdom and maturity for you. If your wounds remain unhealed, they can fester and ultimately erupt, causing you untold pain and heartache throughout your life.

- You may have tried to cover up your wounds—bandage them, if you will—with quick fixes or distractions, but your unhealed wounds will always find a way to surface, usually in unhealthy ways.

- Unhealed wounds from childhood can cause you to harbor guilt, shame, fear, and insecurities deep within your soul that will affect your closest relationships and make it hard for you to connect emotionally.

- If you desire to live authentically and wholly, you need to have the courage to examine your wounds, find ways to heal them, and make conscious changes in your life so you don't pass on those wounds to your children.

- You cannot do the work of healing your past on your own. You need others who can see things about yourself that you may not see. This is a crucial part of your journey.

- This book of daily reflections will help you explore some of the most common wounds men experience in their lives and will provide probing questions to help you recognize them in yourself and to take steps toward healing. It will also point you to the throne of grace, where Jesus sits, and where you may receive His mercy and find His grace to help you in your time of need (Hebrews 4:16).

MY PRAYER FOR YOU IS THAT THIS BOOK OF DAILY REFLECTIONS WILL HELP YOU SEE YOURSELF MORE CLEARLY, UNDERSTAND YOUR STORY MORE COMPLETELY, AND INVITE JESUS INTO THE DEPTHS OF YOUR SOUL DAILY.

Day One

STORY

Your life is a story. It's a story that matters. Some chapters of your life have already been written, while others are waiting to unfold. But here's one of the most amazing things about your story: God is the author. As Romans 11:36 tells us, all things are "from him and through him." That means you're not alone in this journey, and your story has a purpose.

Life can be tough sometimes. We all have our strengths and weaknesses, and we've all been wounded by people or situations along the way. But here's the thing. **Taking the time to understand your story is one of the most important steps you can take toward becoming the man God created you to be.**

It's not always easy to look back and go deep, to see what's behind and beneath it all. But it's worth it. **When you start to understand why you are who you are and why you do the things you do, it's a game-changer.** It will help you in your relationships, your self-awareness, your emotional health, your spiritual health, and in your walk with Jesus.

Scripture tells us that we have choices in life.

- Colossians 2:6–7 encourages us to continue to live our lives in Christ, being strengthened in the faith.

- Philippians 4:6 reminds us to bring our anxieties to God in prayer.

- First Peter 5:7 tells us to cast all our cares on Him because He cares for us.

These verses show us that while God is the author of our story, we have the power to make choices that align with His will for our lives as we add to our own stories.

So here's my challenge to you: take some time each day as you read these daily reflections to pause, ponder, and reflect on your story, where you've been and where you're going in life. Look at yourself for who you really are, with all your strengths and weaknesses, your joys and wounds.

Know that this is a process. These reflections are designed to take you on a journey to see yourself more clearly, understand your story more completely, and invite Jesus into the depths of your soul daily. **You'll find there will be some repetition and redundancy in the reflections, and that is by design. It's a process. It takes practice and repetition. It's a daily choice. For some of you, it will be like learning to play a new sport or play a new instrument.**

You'll also notice in the reflections that this journey isn't linear. It's not a "connect the dots" experience. We'll jump around in the reflections, visiting and revisiting some of the same themes that are common with most men, mixing them up and spreading them out so you can process them over time and have space in between. Again, that is by design.

It's important to note that while each daily reflection draws from the wisdom of Scripture, this book isn't designed to be a Bible study. It's written to be a tool to help take you into your soul, to see yourself more clearly, to be real with yourself and other trusted men, to sit with Jesus, and to help you heal from some of the most common wounds men experience.

Allow yourself to sit in each reflection, to do the work, to repeat yourself, to allow yourself to grow and heal, to see more clearly, and to move toward greater emotional and spiritual health.

> **REFLECTION:** What has surprised you most about your life story so far? Take some time to write about three things in your life story that surprise you most. They can be either good things or bad things. Reflect on how those things affect how you are living your life today. And as you reflect, remember that God is the author of your story, and He has a plan and a purpose for every chapter.

Day Two

SEEKING RENEWAL IN A BROKEN WORLD

Every man's story is part of a greater narrative, one that begins in the Garden of Eden. It's a story of creation, of life breathed into dust, of intimate relationship with our Creator. **But it's also a story of brokenness, of a world marred by sin and suffering.**

We see this brokenness all around us. It's in the headlines that grieve our hearts, the relationships that leave us wounded, the inner turmoil that keeps us awake at night. We live in a world that is beautiful, yes, but also deeply broken.

If we're honest, we recognize that brokenness exists within ourselves too. As much as we might try to have it all together, the truth is, we're all unfinished. We're all works in progress, navigating this life with fractured hearts and fragile hopes.

But here's the good news: our brokenness is not the end of the story. In fact, it's the very place where God meets us with His grace. The apostle Paul puts it this way in 2 Corinthians 4:7–9: "But we have this treasure in jars of clay to show that this all-surpassing power is from God and not from us. We are hard pressed on every side, but not crushed; perplexed, but not in despair; persecuted, but not abandoned; struck down, but not destroyed" (NIV).

As men, we often feel the pressure to be strong, to have all the answers, to never show weakness. **But Paul reminds us that it's in our weakness, in our brokenness, that God's strength shines through.**

5

It's when we come to the end of ourselves that we find the beginning of God's grace.

This doesn't mean that we wallow in our brokenness or use it as an excuse to stay stuck. Rather, it means that we bring our unfinished selves to God, trusting in His power to renew and restore us. It means that we embrace the journey of authentic manhood, knowing that growth and healing are a process. We know it's a daily commitment to let go more, trust Jesus more, be honest with ourselves more, and grow more.

What could this look like for you? It might mean having the courage to be vulnerable with a trusted friend about your struggles. It might mean seeking wise counsel when you're facing a difficult decision. It might mean carving out time each day to be still before God, bringing your broken pieces to Him in prayer.

As you continually seek daily renewal in Christ, you'll find that your brokenness becomes the very place where you experience God's love most profoundly. I think you'll discover that your wounds can become windows for God's light to shine through.

So today, if you find yourself feeling broken, unfinished, or weary, take heart. You are not alone. You are loved by a God who specializes in redeeming broken stories. Bring your authentic self to Him and watch as He works in and through you.

REFLECTION: In what areas of your life do you feel most broken or unfinished? How might God be inviting you to bring those areas to Him for renewal and restoration? What would it look like for you to embrace more vulnerability and community as part of your journey?

FINGER POINTING

As we begin thinking about our life's story, let's talk about the wounds. Our wounds have a profound impact on our story, oftentimes in ways we're not even aware of. You know what I'm talking about when I say "wounds." We all have them even if we're not consciously aware of them. Wounds are those painful experiences from our past we think we've moved on from but somehow keep coming back to haunt us. It's like they're hiding in the back of our minds, waiting for the perfect moment to jump out and catch us off guard.

And when they do, it's usually not pretty. It's like a shaken-up bottle of soda, ready to explode. We're surprised, scared, and then angry. And that's when the finger-pointing can begin.

When we're not aware of and don't understand our wounds, it's easy to start pointing our finger and blaming everyone and everything around us. We think it's someone else's fault for triggering us, but the truth is, we've been nurturing that internal time bomb all along. And when it goes off, we lash out at the people closest to us.

We forget what Scripture tells us in Matthew 7:3–5: "Why do you look at the speck of sawdust in your brother's eye and pay no attention to the plank in your own eye? . . . first take the plank out of your own eye, and then you will see clearly to remove the speck from your brother's eye" (NIV). **We need to take a hard look at ourselves before we start pointing fingers at others.**

I know it's not easy to confront those painful memories and festering wounds. It's like rebreaking a bone that hasn't healed properly. But it's the only way to set ourselves free and keep that poison from seeping into our relationships.

So here's my challenge to you: start uncovering those hiding places. Face down those painful memories and feelings. And if you need to, have those tough conversations with the people who caused them. We'll talk more about that as we go. It takes courage, but with God's help, you can do it. When it feels painful, remind yourself as the apostle Paul did that you can do all things **in Christ** who strengthens you (Philippians 4:13). **In Christ. Invite Jesus into your deepest hiding places. He will meet you in those places with His love and His grace.**

As you reflect, remember that God is with you every step of the way. He knows your wounds, and He wants to heal them. Keep reminding yourself of that truth. Trust in His love and guidance as you do the hard work of confronting your past and setting yourself free for your future.

REFLECTION: Take some time to journal about specific instances when you've been triggered by the words of a loved one and found yourself blaming them. Do you tend to blame others when you feel triggered by guilt or pain? Do you have the courage to relive the pain of your past in order to reset your future?

Day Four

WHEN LIFE HITS YOU IN THE FACE

Has life ever hit you in the face? I mean, really knocked the wind out of you? Maybe it was a phone call with devastating news, a business failure, or a heartbreaking diagnosis. If you haven't experienced this yet, I gently suggest that you likely will at some point. **Life has a way of throwing curveballs when we least expect them.**

As I ponder this life reality for most of us, I reflect on the time when Jesus told His disciples that they would face troubles in this world (John 16:33). I don't think He told them that to discourage them, but to prepare them and to offer them peace. A peace that could only be found in Him, knowing that He had already overcome the things of this world.

In my own story, I've been hit in the face by life more times than I'd like to admit. Each time, it has changed me—not just in my circumstances but in my heart and soul. **It reminds me that my spiritual journey is so much more than just accumulating knowledge about God.** Don't get me wrong, knowledge is important. It's foundational in my own spiritual journey. But when life shatters our ideals and leaves us holding the broken pieces, we need something more.

We need healing. We need to be seen, known, and loved in our messiness and our pain. And that's exactly what Jesus offers us. He meets us in the depths of our stories, in the dark nights of our soul, with a hope that transcends our understanding.

9

When life hits you in the face, remember that Jesus told us troubles would come. But He also promised that we could take heart because He has overcome the world. We don't need to have all the answers or make sense of everything. **We can let go and trust in His love and His care for us.**

This doesn't make the pain disappear, but it does give us an anchor to hold on to. It reminds us that our story, no matter how bruised and broken, is held in the hands of a Savior who knows suffering and offers healing.

So when life knocks you down, reach out to Jesus. Fall into His arms. Sometimes it's helpful for me to picture myself literally falling into His arms. Invite Him into your pain, your confusion, your heartbreak. Let Him meet you there with His comforting presence and transformative love.

And as you walk through the valleys, remember that you are not alone. Many of us have been where you are. We've had to learn to lean on Jesus in new ways, to trust Him with our shattered pieces. In His care, those pieces can become a beautiful mosaic, a testament to His grace and redemption.

Your story, even the chapters that feel dark and hopeless, matters. It's in these chapters that Jesus can shine the brightest, revealing His power to bring beauty from ashes and hope from despair. Remember, you are seen, known, and deeply loved by the One who has overcome the world. Your story, in all its chapters, is in His hands.

REFLECTION: Reflect on a time when life hit you in the face. How did that experience change you—emotionally, spiritually, mentally? In the midst of the pain and confusion, were you able to "take courage" in Jesus? If not, what held you back? Consider bringing this experience to Jesus in prayer, inviting Him to meet you in the hard places and to bring His healing and hope.

Day Five

BIGGER THAN LIFE

For a young boy, his father looms larger than life itself. He is the embodiment of masculinity, the blueprint for how to navigate the world as a man. A boy watches his father intently, absorbing every interaction, every word, every gesture, seeking to understand what it means to be a man, a husband, a father, and a member of society.

When a boy is blessed with a father who is emotionally present, supportive, and loving, he is gifted with a solid foundation on which to build his own identity. Proverbs 22:6 tells us, "Train up a child in the way he should go; even when he is old he will not depart from it." A father who models healthy relationships, deep faith, vulnerability, and self-assurance equips his son with the tools to forge his own path with confidence.

What is your relationship with your dad like? **If your father has been absent, critical, or abusive, you've been deeply wounded by your dad.** You have been left to grapple with a void, a hunger for affection and approval that can color every aspect of your adult life. You may find yourself struggling with intimacy, self-worth, and emotional expression, perpetuating a cycle of pain that ripples through generations.

Scripture is not silent on the importance of a father's role. In Ephesians 6:4, fathers are instructed, "Do not provoke your children to anger, but bring them up in the discipline and instruction of the

11

Lord." A father's words and actions have the power to shape his son's heart, for better or for worse.

As men, we must recognize that our fathers, too, were once little boys, searching for guidance and love. They operated out of their own wounds, their own unmet needs. While this understanding does not excuse hurtful behavior, it can be a starting point for compassion and healing.

The journey toward authentic manhood begins with acknowledging and tending to the **"father wound."** It's that important. It requires a brave and honest look at how our relationship with our dad has influenced our beliefs about ourselves, about masculinity, and about our place in the world.

But we do not undertake this journey alone. Our Heavenly Father is ready to meet us in our pain, to offer the unconditional love and acceptance we crave. Psalm 68:5 reminds us, "Father of the fatherless . . . is God in his holy habitation." In His love, we find the strength to break unhealthy patterns, to extend forgiveness to our dad, and to become the father we long to be for our own family.

REFLECTION: Reflect on your relationship with your dad. How has it shaped your understanding of manhood? Do you harbor resentment or blame toward him? Can you begin to see him as a man with his own wounds and struggles? Pray for wisdom and grace as you consider how to break negative cycles in your own role as a father or mentor.

Day Six

THE INFLUENCE OF MOM

A son's relationship with his mom is truly special. From the moment of conception, a deep connection is formed that has the potential to shape a boy's emotional landscape for a lifetime. **When a son is blessed with a healthy, nurturing relationship with his mom, he's been given an incredible gift.**

Proverbs 31:25–28 paints a beautiful picture of a godly mother: "Strength and dignity are her clothing, and she laughs at the time to come. She opens her mouth with wisdom, and the teaching of kindness is on her tongue. She looks well to the ways of her household and does not eat the bread of idleness. Her children rise up and call her blessed; her husband also, and he praises her." A mother who embodies these qualities—who affirms her son's identity, delights in his presence, encourages his growth, and comforts him in times of need—lays a foundation of security and confidence that will serve him well in his future relationships.

However, just like with dads, it's important to recognize that no mom is perfect. **Even the most well-intentioned mom brings her own baggage and wounds into her parenting, and these can't help but affect her son in some way.** Romans 3:23 reminds us that we all sin and fall short of perfection. While a mom's love may be deep and genuine, it is not flawless.

If you've experienced a more challenging relationship with your mom—one marked by control, neglect, or abuse—you've

13

been deeply wounded by your mom. Trust may be difficult for you to cultivate, both in yourself and in others. The shadow of this maternal wound can loom large, influencing your interactions with women and your overall sense of emotional security.

Scripture gives us a beautiful example of God working through a well-meaning, but imperfect, mom and grandmother to perpetuate a deep faith in the life of their son and grandson, Timothy. Paul writes in 2 Timothy 1:5 of Timothy and his heritage: "I am reminded of your sincere faith, a faith that dwelt first in your grandmother Lois and your mother Eunice and now, I am sure, dwells in you as well." Despite the challenges Timothy likely faced in his upbringing, the faith and influence of his mother and grandmother had a profound impact on his life and ministry.

As you reflect on your relationship with your mom, it's crucial to approach your exploration with grace and wisdom. Acknowledging the impact of this bond—both its blessings and its challenges—and growing in your awareness of your own personal journey with your mom is critical in better understanding your story . . . in explaining you to you.

> **REFLECTION:** Take some time to prayerfully consider your relationship with your mom. What aspects of this bond do you cherish and appreciate? Are there areas of pain or unresolved hurt that may be affecting your current relationships? Bring these reflections before God, asking for His perspective and His healing touch. If you discern a need for deeper exploration or healing in this area, consider seeking the support of a trusted counselor or spiritual mentor.

BREAKING FREE FROM THE "ALL-ALONE WOUND"

The "all-alone wound" can be a heavy burden to bear, causing you to isolate yourself and avoid the very relationships that have the power to bring healing and joy. You were never meant to do life alone.

In Galatians 6:2, Paul urges us to "bear one another's burdens, and so fulfill the law of Christ." We were created for interdependence, for the mutual support and encouragement that comes from doing life together.

When you allow the all-alone wound to be a main driver in your story, you're not only robbing yourself of the deep fulfillment that comes from loving and being loved, but you're also denying others the gift of knowing and supporting you.

It's easy to pour yourself into work, hobbies, or surface-level acquaintances as a way of avoiding the vulnerability that true connection requires. But as Ecclesiastes 4:9–10 reminds us, "Two are better than one, because they have a good reward for their toil. For if they fall, one will lift up his fellow." When you have people in your corner who truly see and understand you, who can offer you the much-needed encouragement we all need, you're better equipped to face life's challenges and to grow into the man God created you to be.

If you find yourself connected but alone, a good way to begin breaking free from the all-alone wound is with a willingness to examine your heart, to bring your fears and insecurities into the light of God's love. In Psalm 139:23–24, David prays, "Search me, O God, and know my heart! Try me and know my thoughts! And see if there be any grievous way in me, and lead me in the way everlasting!" When you invite God into your journey of healing, He can begin to reveal the thought patterns and beliefs that have kept you isolated, replacing them with the truth of His unwavering love and acceptance.

From this place of security in God's love, you can begin to take small steps toward cultivating deeper relationships. This might mean opening up to your spouse more about your struggles, joining a men's group, or reaching out to a trusted friend for support. As you practice vulnerability and allow others to see the real you, you'll find that the all-alone wound begins to lose its power.

Building meaningful relationships takes time, effort, and a willingness to push through discomfort. But as you invest in the people around you and allow them to invest in you, you'll discover a richness and purpose that far outweigh the temporary safety of isolation. You'll find that life's greatest joys and deepest growth often happen in the context of loving, supportive relationships.

REFLECTION: Take a moment to prayerfully consider any ways in which the all-alone wound may be affecting your life. Are there relationships you've been avoiding out of fear or insecurity? What is one small step you can take this week to cultivate deeper connection with someone in your life?

TAKING THE FIRST STEP TOWARD HEALING

As a man, it's easy to try and ignore the wounds that stem from your relationship with your mom and dad. You might feel a natural inclination to push aside the pain, to convince yourself that it doesn't matter or that it will simply fade away with time. But the truth is, these wounds have a profound impact on who you are as a man, and they deserve your attention and care.

Your heart, the center of your emotional and spiritual life, is deeply influenced by your early experiences and relationships. When left unaddressed, the wounds from your past will shape your present in ways you might not even realize.

Healing wounds from our early life is an essential part of every man's journey to authentic manhood. It requires awareness, commitment, time, and a willingness to confront the difficult things in your life. As Psalm 147:3 assures us, "He heals the brokenhearted and binds up their wounds." God desires to walk with you in this process, to bring His healing touch to the deepest parts of your soul.

Taking the first step toward healing can feel daunting, but it's a step worth taking. It's a decision to prioritize your emotional and spiritual well-being, to invest in your own growth and wholeness. As you embark on this journey, remember the words of James 1:4: "Let perseverance finish its work so that you may be mature and com-

17

plete, not lacking anything" (NIV). The process of healing may not be quick or easy, but it leads to a more fulfilling and authentic life.

God, in His wisdom, has given us the gift of time in the healing process. Just as physical wounds require time to heal, so do emotional and spiritual wounds. Rushing the process or expecting instant results can lead to frustration and discouragement. Instead, embrace the journey and trust in God's timing.

Consider, too, the impact your healing can have on those around you. When you choose to ignore your wounds, you risk passing on that same pain to your children or others close to you. But when you courageously face your past and allow God to transform your pain, you break the cycle. You become a conduit of healing and hope for the next generation. Be confident that He who began a good work in you will carry it to completion in Christ (Philippians 1:6).

Start by acknowledging your need for healing. Bring your wounds before God in honest prayer, asking Him to reveal the areas that need His restorative touch. Seek out trusted friends, mentors, or counselors who can walk alongside you in this process. Remember, "Two are better than one, because they have a good return for their labor: If either of them falls down, one can help the other up" (Ecclesiastes 4:9–10 NIV).

REFLECTION: What wounds from your past have you been hesitant to address? How might these wounds be affecting your life and relationships in the present? What fears or hesitations do you have about embarking on this process of healing? Pray for the courage to take that first step and the wisdom to seek out the support you need along the way.

Day Nine

IT'S COMPLICATED

"It's complicated." Those two words often describe a boy's relationship with his dad, especially when that dad is physically or emotionally absent. The title itself suggests a tangled web of emotions, a knot that can feel impossible to unravel.

When a father is physically absent, the void is tangible. But an emotionally absent father, while physically present, can leave just as deep a wound. A boy in this situation may have a guide but not a confidant. He may have a provider but not a nurturer. **The result can be a complicated mix of longing, confusion, and self-doubt.**

A boy with an absent father, whether physically or emotionally, often internalizes that absence as a reflection of his own worth. He may question what he did to drive his father away or what he could have done to make him stay. This self-doubt can color his entire identity, leading to a complicated relationship with himself and others.

As he grows into a man, this "father wound" can manifest in various ways. He may find it difficult to trust, always anticipating abandonment. He may struggle with intimacy, fearing vulnerability. Or he may seek validation in unhealthy ways, attempting to fill the father-shaped hole in his heart.

Healing from a relationship that never fully existed is a complex journey. It begins with acknowledging the wound and understanding its impact. It requires learning to extend compassion and

19

love to yourself, a task that can feel foreign if you have always felt unworthy of love from your dad.

But there is hope. In Psalm 27:10, David writes, "Though my father and mother forsake me, the LORD will receive me" (NIV). **Our Heavenly Father is ready to meet you in your pain, to offer the unconditional love and acceptance you crave.** In His love, you can begin to untangle the complicated knot of your father wound.

Remember, healing is a journey, and you don't walk it alone. Lean into the love of your Heavenly Father, and trust in His ability to bring wholeness to even the most complicated of wounds.

REFLECTION: Reflect on your relationship with your dad. Was he available to you physically, mentally, and emotionally? Do you harbor complicated feelings toward him? Take a moment to bring those feelings to your Heavenly Father. Ask Him to help you extend compassion to yourself and to give you wisdom as you navigate the impact of your father wound on your relationships with others.

Day Ten

WALKING THE TIGHTROPE

Growing up with an emotionally unpredictable mom can feel like walking a tightrope. One moment she's nurturing, the next she's cold or even cruel. This inconsistency can leave you constantly on edge, always trying to gauge her mood and adjust your behavior accordingly. You learn to stay hypervigilant, ready to either fight or flee at a moment's notice.

While this survival mechanism may have served you well in childhood, it can wreak havoc on your adult relationships, especially with women. When you've grown up with an unstable maternal figure, learning to trust can feel like a daunting task.

You may find yourself constantly waiting for the other shoe to drop, even in healthy relationships. **Minor disagreements or changes in your partner's mood can trigger that old fight-or-flight response, leaving you anxious and on guard.** This chronic state of anxiety can erode the very intimacy and connection you crave.

In Philippians 4:6–7, we're encouraged to not be anxious about anything but, instead, to pray about everything. We can enjoy the peace of God, even in the midst of broken and hard relationships. When you are continually bringing your relationship anxieties to God in prayer, He can bring peace to your heart and even begin to heal those deep-seated wounds, replacing fear with faith.

21

Learning to trust when you've grown up with an emotionally unhealthy mom is a process, one that requires patience and self-compassion. As you navigate new relationships, give yourself permission to take things slowly. Pay attention to the consistency and reliability of those around you, and cautiously allow yourself to lean into that stability. When anxiety arises, take a moment to breathe, pray, and remind yourself that you are safe and loved by a God who never changes. Seek your peace from Him.

It's also important to communicate openly with your family about your struggle with trusting others. Sharing your story and your triggers can help them understand and support you better. Together, you can create a relationship dynamic that feels safe and secure, one that allows you to step off the tightrope and into the freedom of genuine connection.

Remember, your worth is not defined by your past or your struggles. You've been assured that if you're in Christ, you're a new creation. Trust that God is working in your life to heal your wounds and lead you toward healthier, more fulfilling relationships.

REFLECTION: Reflect on how your relationship with your mom may be affecting your current relationships. Do you find yourself constantly on high alert, waiting for disappointment or rejection? Take these fears to God in prayer, asking Him to replace them with His perfect love. If you're in a relationship, consider sharing your struggles with your partner and brainstorming ways to create a more secure and stable dynamic. If you're not in a relationship, think about the qualities you want in a future partner—consistency, reliability, emotional stability. Trust that God can lead you to a relationship that reflects His unchanging love.

STRENGTH IN VULNERABILITY

As men, we often feel the pressure to present a strong, unflappable exterior to the world. Society has conditioned us to believe that expressing our emotions or admitting our struggles is a sign of weakness. We put on a brave face, even as we privately wrestle with our doubts, fears, and wounds.

But what if true strength lies not in hiding our vulnerabilities but in having the courage to share them? The apostle Paul tells us that our power is made perfect in weakness when we have the power of Christ in us (2 Corinthians 12:9). **When we're willing to acknowledge our struggles, we open ourselves up to the transformative power of God's grace.**

Consider the example of David, a man after God's own heart. Throughout the psalms, he pours out his heart to God, expressing the full range of human emotions—fear, anger, despair, joy, and hope. In doing so, he finds strength, comfort, and direction. As men, we can learn from David's example, bringing our authentic selves before God and trusted others.

Imagine the freedom and energy that could be unleashed in our lives if we no longer had to expend so much effort in keeping up appearances. Instead of isolating ourselves in our struggles, we could find strength in community.

This kind of vulnerable, supportive community doesn't happen by accident. It requires intentionality, courage, and a willingness to go first. It might mean initiating a deeper conversation with a friend, joining a men's group, or seeking out a mentor. As we take those steps, we create space for authentic connection and growth.

Finding yourself at a place in life in which you may be exceedingly connected with others on the surface, but all alone inside, doesn't have to define who you are or be your endgame. It can simply be part of your story, a story that God can use for your good and His glory. **Take a step toward embracing vulnerability in this season of your life.** Lean into the support of others. You'll find that your inner battles begin to lose their power. You'll discover a new kind of strength—the strength that comes from living authentically, in the light of God's love and grace.

> **REFLECTION:** Take a moment to consider your own comfort level with vulnerability. Are there areas of your life where you've been hesitant to share your struggles? What holds you back? Pray for the courage to take a step toward authentic sharing with a trusted friend or group this week. Remember, you don't have to have it all together. Your willingness to be real is a gift to yourself and to those around you.

Day Twelve

ROOTED IN THE MIDST OF LIFE'S STORMS

Have you ever seen a tumbleweed aimlessly rolling around on the ground through the desert? Just a small, dry bundle of twigs being randomly tossed about by the wind. I've had moments in my life when I've felt like a tumbleweed being tossed around by life.

Maybe you can relate. As men, we can face a lot of challenges— in our careers, in our relationships, in our own hearts and minds. And sometimes, it can feel like we're just being randomly tossed around by the circumstances of life.

The thing about tumbleweeds is that they have no root system. There's nothing to nourish them or anchor them when the winds pick up. And I think that's a pretty good picture of what happens to us when we try to navigate life on our own strength.

Scripture talks about this in Ephesians 4:14, where it describes people who are "tossed back and forth by the waves, and blown here and there by every wind of teaching" (NIV). That's what happens when we don't have a firm foundation. We get easily confused, easily led astray.

But here's the good news: **God never intended for us to live like tumbleweeds. He created us for a deep, life-giving connection**

with Him. A connection that can provide us with roots no matter what storms come our way.

In Colossians 2:6–7, we find this incredible invitation: "Therefore, as you received Christ Jesus the Lord, **so walk in him**, rooted and built up in him and established in the faith, just as you were taught, abounding in thanksgiving." **Walk in and be rooted in Christ.** We're invited to let Him be our strength, our stability. As a follower of Jesus, our very life is found in Him.

Sometimes it may feel like that's easier said than done when we're carrying around a bunch of deep wounds, when our hearts feel broken and scarred. It's tempting to think that we need to have it all together before we can come to God.

But the beautiful thing about the gospel is that Jesus meets us right where we are. He's not surprised by our brokenness. He's not put off by our wounds. In fact, He specializes in redeeming and restoring the broken places in our lives.

Remember, when the prodigal son came home after squandering his inheritance, his father didn't demand that he get cleaned up first. He ran to him, embraced him, and celebrated his return. That's how our Heavenly Father feels about us.

Sink your roots deep into the love of Christ. Draw your nourishment and strength from Him. When the winds of life blow, you can stand strong, not because of your own strength but because of the One who provides you with roots.

This doesn't mean you won't face challenges. It doesn't mean life will always be easy. **But it does mean that in the midst of the storms, you have a hope that holds.** You have a peace that can't be shaken. You have a joy that's not dependent on your circumstances.

Today, right where you are standing in your story, **if you're feeling more like a tumbleweed than a deeply rooted tree, remember**

this: You are loved by a God who is in the business of bringing life from death, hope from despair, and beauty from ashes. Turn to Him. Trust in Him. Let His love be the soil in which you grow.

> **REFLECTION:** Take a moment to consider where you've been looking for stability and strength. Have you been relying on your own abilities, your own wisdom? How might your life look different if you were truly rooted and built up in Christ? What's one meaningful way you can sink your roots deeper into His love today?

SEEING BEYOND YOUR BLIND SPOTS

We all have blind spots—aspects of our life, behavior, and reactions that we may not be fully aware of. Your blind spots will shape your story. Just as drivers must be cautious of areas outside their peripheral vision, you must be willing to acknowledge that there are parts of yourself that others may see more clearly than you do, and if you don't work on seeing them, you could get off track.

Jeremiah 17:9 reminds us that "the heart is deceitful above all things and beyond cure. Who can understand it?" (NIV). Our own perceptions of ourselves can be skewed, shaped by our experiences, wounds, and self-protective mechanisms.

Some of your blind spots are rooted in unhealed wounds from your boyhood. The impact of these early experiences can be profound, shaping your thoughts, emotions, and behaviors in ways you might not even recognize. As Proverbs 20:5 observes, "The purposes of a person's heart are deep waters, but one who has insight draws them out" (NIV).

Inviting trusted others to speak into your life can be a powerful tool for growth and healing. They may see strengths and gifts in you that you've overlooked due to self-criticism. They may also gently point out patterns or reactions that stem from past hurts, helping you to bring these areas to light for healing.

This process requires humility and vulnerability. It means being open to feedback, even when it's uncomfortable. Proverbs 27:17 assures us, "Iron sharpens iron, and one man sharpens another." When we allow others to help us see our blind spots, we open the door to personal growth and transformation.

Of course, it's important to choose your confidants wisely. Look for people who have your best interests at heart, who will speak truth to you in love, and who will support you in your journey of growth. Proverbs 12:26 advises, "The righteous choose their friends carefully, but the way of the wicked leads them astray" (NIV).

As you become more aware of your own blind spots, you'll develop a greater capacity to extend grace and understanding to others. You'll recognize that everyone is on their own journey, navigating their own challenges and growth areas. By supporting and encouraging one another, you create a community of healing and transformation.

> **REFLECTION:** Take a moment to consider your own blind spots. Are there areas of your life where you suspect you might not see yourself as clearly as others do? Ask God to give you a humble and open heart, ready to receive the insights and support of trusted others. Consider initiating a conversation with a friend, family member, or mentor, asking them to share what they see as your strengths and growth areas. The goal is not perfection but rather a commitment to ongoing growth and healing.

AUTHENTICITY IN THE FACE OF LOSS

Loss is a part of our story. Loss is a part of life. Whether it's the loss of a loved one, a job, a dream, or a sense of self, we all experience it at some point. And it can be hard. It can make us feel like we've been punched in the gut, leaving us sad, exhausted, and confused.

I've experienced great loss. There was a season in my life when I lost both of my parents and my younger brother within a span of a few years. My entire childhood family, gone. It changed me. For a season, I was listless and depressed. **I went from being the guy with the answers who was ready to take on the day, solve everybody's problems, achieve great things, and charge forward to the next hill, to feeling like a shell of myself.**

One day, I was sitting with a mentor of mine, Jack, and I asked him, "When will I get the old Steve back? The Steve who was excited about life, engaged, driven. How long will it take to get him back?"

Jack's response surprised me. After a long, meaningful pause, he said, **"I kind of like this new Steve better."** What? You like this new Steve better? How? I feel like a shell of myself. He went on to explain, **"Well, that old Steve, he kind of 'had it all together.'"**

His words hit me hard. Over the next weeks and months, his wisdom settled in. I began to see what he was saying. My eyes were opened to see in a new way. I had spent so much of my life trying to act like I had it all figured out, even in my spiritual life—maybe *especially* in my spiritual life. **But the truth is, none of us has all the answers**

or has it all figured out. We're all on this journey of life, learning and growing and stumbling along the way. And that's okay. In fact, it's more than okay. It's exactly how it's supposed to be.

The apostle Paul understood this. In 2 Corinthians 12:9–10, he writes, "**But he said to me, 'My grace is sufficient for you, for my power is made perfect in weakness.'** Therefore I will boast all the more gladly about my weaknesses, so that the power of Christ may rest upon me. For the sake of Christ, then, I am content with weaknesses, insults, hardships, persecutions, and calamities. For when I am weak, then I am strong."

When we let go of the need to have it all together, we open ourselves up to a deeper relationship with Jesus. **We learn to truly need Him, not just know about Him.** We learn to be with Him, breath by breath, moment by moment.

This is the heart of authentic manhood—not having all the answers but being real about our struggles and our need for God and others. It's about inviting Jesus into our pain, our confusion, and our loss, and allowing Him to meet us there with His love and grace. It's about walking with each other through the good, the bad, and the ugly, knowing that we're all in this together.

So if you're facing loss or hardship, know that you're not alone. If you're sitting in unhealed wounds from long ago**, you don't have to put on a brave face or act like you have it all figured out. Instead, lean into Jesus**. Let Him be your strength in weakness, your comfort in sorrow, your hope in despair. And let others in too. Share your story, your struggles, your heart. It's in this authenticity that you can find true freedom and healing in Christ.

REFLECTION: Think about a time when you faced a significant loss or hardship. How did you respond? Did you feel pressure to "have it all together," or were you able to be real about your struggles? What might it look like for you to invite Jesus into that pain and to share your authentic self with others? Remember, in Christ you are loved and accepted just as you are, weaknesses and all.

Day Fifteen

THE ART OF SHAPING GLASS

Have you ever watched a glass artisan at work? It's a beautiful process, but it requires a gentle hand and a lot of patience. The artisan has to keep the glass heated in a furnace to make it malleable. If the glass cools down, it becomes brittle and impossible to shape.

Our hearts work like this too. **We need a constant source of love and grace to keep our hearts soft and open to healing and change.** And there's nothing more powerful in doing that than the love and grace of Jesus.

When we invite Jesus into our story, He walks with us every step of the way. In John 10:9, Jesus says, "I am the door. If anyone enters by me, he will be saved and will go in and out and find pasture." That pasture is the nourishment our hearts need.

When we're in Christ, we become a new creation (2 Corinthians 5:17). Jesus knows us better than we know ourselves. He sees where we need to change, grow, and be reshaped. And He's ready to help us do just that.

It starts with you allowing the constant presence of Jesus's love and grace into your heart. It's about receiving His love and grace so that you can extend that same love and grace to others—and to yourself. That's what softens your heart and enables you to do the hard work of healing, forgiveness, and transformation.

Throughout Scripture, we see Jesus healing and reshaping the hearts of all kinds of men—tax collectors, fishermen, blind men, doubters, argumentative men, sick men, and even thieves. One of the apostle Paul's prayers in Ephesians 1:18 was that the people would have "the eyes of your hearts enlightened, that you may know what is the hope to which he has called you."

God knows how to reshape your life into the masterpiece He created you to be. Trust in His love, grace, and gentle guidance as you embark on this transformative journey.

REFLECTION: Take some time for soul-searching with this reflection. Have you fully submitted your life to Jesus, placing your future in His hands and asking Him to heal your pain? Are you all in with Jesus, giving Him full access to your heart? Are you willing to go through the patient process it may take to reframe your past and fully transform your life?

Day Sixteen

THE RESTLESS SOUL

For a man carrying the weight of an unresolved father wound, the quiet of the night can be a treacherous place. During the day, he may find solace in the busyness of life, masking his pain with the distractions of work and responsibilities. But as the world stills and the noise fades, the ghosts of his past emerge, haunting his thoughts and stealing his peace.

Scripture speaks of the importance of dealing with anger and hurt, warning us in Ephesians 4:26–27, "Be angry and do not sin; do not let the sun go down on your anger, and give no opportunity to the devil." If you are harboring hidden resentment toward your father, be it for physical or emotional absence, you are unwittingly allowing that bitterness to take root in your soul.

Over time, this unresolved pain can manifest in various ways. You may struggle with self-doubt, questioning your worth and abilities. You may find yourself stuck in a cycle of guilt and shame, unable to extend grace and forgiveness to yourself. These feelings can be especially pronounced in the solitude of the night when there are no distractions to drown out the voice of your wounded heart.

This inner turmoil can take a toll on your heart. **Holding onto anger and hurt is a heavy burden, one that can sap your vitality and joy.**

But there is hope. The path to healing begins with vulnerability, with a willingness to open up the walls of your heart and examine

35

what lies within. It requires confronting painful memories and long-buried emotions. But it is a necessary step toward quieting your restless soul.

Jesus offers a profound invitation: **"Come to me, all who labor and are heavy laden, and I will give you rest"** (Matthew 11:28). When we bring our father wounds to the feet of our Heavenly Father, we open ourselves to the healing power of His love. Through prayer, through the support of trusted friends or counselors, and through the transformative power of forgiveness, the restless soul can find peace.

Remember, you are not alone in this journey. Your Heavenly Father sees your pain and yearns to bring you peace even in the quiet of the night. Trust in His love and take courage in the knowledge that healing is possible.

REFLECTION: Take a moment to reflect on your own inner world. Do you struggle with anxiety, insecurity, or unwanted memories, particularly in the quiet of the night? What past hurts or unresolved issues might be fueling these feelings?

EFFECTS OF A MOTHER WOUND

It's crucial to understand the impact your relationship with your mom can have on you as a man and how it can leave you with what we're calling a **"mother wound."** Remember, this isn't a bash on moms. But just like our human dads, none of our moms are perfect. They may be wonderful, or they may not be, but either way, they are imperfect humans just like we are.

Our moms play a huge role in shaping who we become. When that relationship is healthy and nurturing, it gives us a solid foundation to build on. But when it's marked by unhealthy dynamics, it can create some real challenges in how we relate to others, especially women.

The mother wound can manifest in a couple of common ways. **First, it can show up as what we'll call the "dominant male."** If you grew up with an overly controlling mom, you might have learned to see women as a threat to your independence. As a result, you may find yourself trying to control the women in your life, keeping them at a distance emotionally. Deep down, there's a fear that getting too close will mean losing yourself.

On the other hand, if your mom did everything for you, you might have become what's known as a "soft male." You might find yourself looking for a girlfriend or a wife to take care of you the way your mom did. You may tend to be passive in your relationships,

37

shying away from making tough decisions or taking risks. While this might come across as sensitivity at first, over time it can lead to a lot of frustration for the women in your life.

Neither of these extremes (dominant or soft) is what God has in mind for us as men. In Ephesians 5:25, which is in the context of marriage, we men are called to love our wives like Christ loves the church—with a selfless, sacrificial love that puts the other person first. It's a love that serves, that leads with compassion and with strength.

But how do we get there if we're carrying around mother wounds? The first step is awareness. Take an honest look at your patterns in relationships, especially with women. Do you tend toward being controlling or passive? Could these tendencies be rooted in your experiences with your mom?

Again, this isn't about placing blame. It's about understanding ourselves more deeply so we can start to break free from the unhealthy patterns we've learned.

That's where the healing power of Christ comes in. As we bring our wounds to Him, as we allow Him to rewire our hearts and minds, we begin to experience transformation from the inside out. It's a process, one that requires vulnerability, humility, and a willingness to grow. But as we surrender to His healing work, inviting Him into the depths of our soul, seeking Him and praying to Him daily, we find ourselves becoming more of the man He created us to be—a man who can reflect the heart of Christ to the world.

If you're recognizing the impact of the mother wound in your own life, take heart. You're not doomed to stay stuck in these patterns. With God's help, and perhaps the support of trusted friends or counselors, you can begin to break free and step into a new way of relating. It begins with seeing yourself clearly and becoming aware.

It's all part of the journey of authentic manhood—a journey that's not always easy but is always worth it. And the beautiful thing is, we get to walk this path together, spurring each other on, pointing each other to the One who heals, restores, and redeems.

> **REFLECTION:** Continue spending some time prayerfully reflecting on your relationship with your mom and how it may be affecting your patterns of relating, especially to women. Ask God to reveal any areas where the mother wound may be influencing your thoughts, emotions, or behaviors. Consider reaching out to a trusted friend or mentor for support and accountability as you walk this path. Remember, in Christ you have the power to break free from the wounds of the past and step into the fullness of the man He's called you to be.

Day Eighteen

THE PERFECTIONIST'S JOURNEY TO GRACE AND HEALING

In a world that often equates worth with performance, it's easy to fall into the trap of perfectionism. We set impossibly high standards for ourselves, believing that if we can just control every aspect of our lives, we'll find the acceptance and love we crave. **But perfectionism is a harsh taskmaster, leaving us exhausted, frustrated, and forever falling short.**

The truth is, perfectionism often stems from deep wounds and insecurities. When we've been hurt by imperfect parents, disloyal friends, or a broken world, we may seek to protect ourselves by striving for flawlessness. We think that if we just can be good enough, we'll be safe from further pain.

But as the apostle Paul reminds us in Romans 3:23–24, "for all have sinned and fall short of the glory of God, and are justified by his grace as a gift, through the redemption that is in Christ Jesus." It's good to continuously remind ourselves that **our worth is not based on our performance but on the infinite love and grace of God.**

When we're trapped in perfectionism, we often project our impossible standards onto others, setting ourselves up for constant disappointment. We become rigid and controlling, unable to adapt or extend grace. This can strain our relationships and reinforce our negative self-talk.

But imagine the freedom that comes from embracing our humanity, from accepting that we're all works in progress. When we allow ourselves to be real, to be the imperfect but beloved children God created us to be, we open ourselves up to authentic connection and growth.

This doesn't mean that we stop striving for excellence or that we make excuses for harmful behavior. But it does mean that we learn to extend the same grace and compassion to ourselves that we would to a dear friend. It means that we trust in God's love and in the love of those who see our worth beyond our achievements.

Philippians 1:6 offers this encouragement: "And I am sure of this, that he who began a good work in you will bring it to completion at the day of Jesus Christ." Our growth and healing is a journey, and God is with us every step of the way.

Practical steps for letting go of perfectionism might include the following:

- Practice self-compassion by speaking to yourself with kindness and understanding and seeing yourself through the eyes of Jesus and His unconditional love for you.

- Set realistic, achievable goals, and celebrate progress over perfection.

- Cultivate hobbies or activities you can enjoy without having to be perfect at them.

- Surround yourself with people who love and accept you unconditionally.

- Regularly remind yourself of your identity as a beloved child of God.

As you begin to loosen the grip of perfectionism, you'll find a new sense of freedom and joy. You'll be able to take risks, to learn from failures, and to invest fully in the imperfect but beautiful relationships in your life. You'll discover that a life of meaning and passion is not about having it all together and being perfect all the time.

REFLECTION: Take a moment to consider how perfectionism may be affecting your life and relationships. Where do you tend to be the hardest on yourself? How might extending grace and compassion to yourself change the way you approach your day-to-day life? Ask God to help you see yourself through His eyes of unconditional love and to guide you in your journey toward embracing your authentic, imperfect self.

Day Nineteen

BEING A LIFE-GIVING SPIRIT

From the moment of Adam's first sin, the human heart has been tainted. We all inherited a natural inclination toward selfishness, a brokenness that can feel impossible to overcome on our own. But here's the good news: when we have Christ in us, we have the power to live differently. We can become life-giving spirits to those around us, not because of our own goodness, but because of His goodness in us.

The apostle Paul puts it this way in 1 Corinthians 15:45: "Thus it is written, 'The first man Adam became a living being'; the last Adam became a life-giving spirit." Jesus, the last Adam, came to restore what was broken in the first Adam. Through His life, death, and resurrection, He offers us a new way to live.

So what does it look like to be a life-giving spirit? It means that in every area of our lives—our careers, our families, our friendships, our communities—we seek to bring life, hope, and healing. We look for opportunities to encourage, to serve, to build others up.

Think about your own career. Whether you're just starting out in your first job or you've been in your field for decades, you have daily opportunities to be a life-giving presence. It might be as simple as offering a word of encouragement to a struggling colleague or going out of your way to help a customer. It might mean praying with your coworkers for their specific needs or mentoring a younger employee.

In your family, being a life-giving spirit means investing in your relationships. It means being present, attentive, and engaged. It means creating an atmosphere of love, safety, and growth in your home.

With your friends, it means being the kind of person who listens, who empathizes, who speaks truth in love. It means celebrating their successes and standing with them in their struggles.

In your community, it means looking for ways to serve, to meet needs, to bring hope. It might mean volunteering for people in need or being a positive influence for the kids you're coaching on a youth sports team.

In all of these areas, Jesus is our model. Throughout the Gospels, we see Him touching lives, healing hurts, and offering hope to everyone He encountered. He didn't discriminate based on social status, gender, or reputation. He gave life to the least of these and to the most influential. He loved those who followed Him as well as those who opposed Him.

As men seeking to live authentic lives, we're called to follow in His footsteps. It's not about trying to muster up enough goodness on our own. It's about staying connected to the source of life Himself. He tells us in John 15:5, "I am the vine; you are the branches. Whoever abides in me and I in him, he it is that bears much fruit, for apart from me you can do nothing."

When we abide in Christ, when we let His life flow through us, we naturally become life-giving spirits. His love, His grace, His compassion can flow out of us, touching and transforming the lives around us.

This is the heart of authentic manhood. It's not about having it all together or achieving some unreachable standard. It's about letting Christ heal our brokenness and using us to heal the brokenness in the world. It's about living each day with the purpose of bringing life to others wherever we go.

> **REFLECTION:** Consider the various areas of your life—your work, your family, your friendships, your community. Where do you see opportunities to be a life-giving spirit? What might it look like for you to bring the life of Christ into those spaces? Remember, it's not about perfection but about daily abiding in Him and letting His life flow through you.

EMBRACING THE DARK NIGHT OF THE SOUL

In your journey of healing, there may come a time when you find yourself in what's known as the "dark night of the soul"—a period of spiritual dryness, doubt, and a sense of distance from God. This experience can be unsettling and even frightening, but it can also be a crucial part of the growth process.

St. John of the Cross, a sixteenth-century Spanish mystic, coined the term **"dark night of the soul"** to describe the spiritual crisis that often precedes significant growth and transformation. He saw it as a necessary purification, a stripping away of our attachments and false selves to make room for a deeper union with God.

In these dark moments, it's essential to remember that God has not abandoned you. As Psalm 23:4 assures, "Even though I walk through the valley of the shadow of death, I will fear no evil, for you are with me; your rod and staff, they comfort me." God is present even in the midst of your struggle, guiding you toward greater wholeness.

Embracing the dark night of the soul is part of the healing process. It means leaning into the discomfort, trusting that healing and growth is happening even when you can't see or feel it. It means being patient with yourself and with the process, knowing that transformation takes time.

Healing is learning. As you do the work of healing, you gain wisdom and resilience. Your scars become badges of honor, testaments to what you've overcome and the growth you've experienced. As Romans 5:3–4 encourages, "Not only so, but we also glory in our sufferings, because we know that suffering produces perseverance; perseverance, character; and character, hope" (NIV).

Embracing the healing process is a deep commitment to your own well-being, your relationships, and your future. It's helping write your story. It means being honest about your pain, seeking support when needed, and trusting in God's ability to bring restoration. Psalm 147:3 says that, "He heals the brokenhearted and binds up their wounds."

> **REFLECTION:** Have you experienced a "dark night of the soul" in your own journey? How did you navigate that season, and what did you learn about yourself and about God in the process? If you find yourself in a dark night currently, don't endure it alone. Invite Jesus in and let others around you love you through it.

THE GREAT PARADOX OF DEATH AND RESURRECTION

As we continue focusing on our story and our journey toward authentic manhood, we often focus on living life fully, living purposefully, living joyfully. I hope for each of those in my life, as I'm sure you do as well. **But we also need to talk about death. Death is part of life.** And there's a profound truth that Jesus teaches us about death with His life: to truly live, we must first die. **It's a paradox that runs counter to our natural inclinations, but it has the power to transform us from the inside out.**

When Jesus calls us to carry our own cross (Matthew 16:24; Mark 8:34; Luke 14:27), **He's inviting us into a life of surrender.** He's asking us to die to our old selves—our selfish desires, our need for control, our pride and ego—so that we can be resurrected into new life in Him.

The apostle Paul understood this deeply. In Galatians 2:20, he writes, "I have been crucified with Christ. It is no longer I who live, but Christ who lives in me. And the life I now live in the flesh I live by faith in the Son of God, who loved me and gave himself for me." **Paul recognized that his old life had to die in order for Christ's life to flourish within him.**

This death and resurrection is not a one-time event but a daily choice. Every day, we're faced with opportunities to die to ourselves—to choose patience over anger, generosity over selfishness, humility over pride. And every time we make that choice, we experience a little resurrection. We discover a new freedom, a new joy, a new sense of purpose.

In our own stories, we may find ourselves clinging to things that are actually holding us back from true life. It might be a grudge we're holding on to, a fear that's paralyzing us, or a pattern of behavior that's destructive. Letting these things die can be scary. It can feel like a risk. But it's in this letting go that we create space for God to do a new work in us.

Think about a seed. For a seed to sprout and grow into a plant, it first has to die. It has to be buried in the dark, damp soil. It has to let go of its old form in order to take on a new one. And when it does, it emerges transformed, reaching toward the sun, bearing fruit.

This is the hope and the promise of following Christ. **As we die to ourselves, as we allow God to prune away everything that's not of Him, we become more fully alive than we ever thought possible.** It's in Christ that the Holy Spirit takes up residence in our life and develops the fruit of the Spirit—love, joy, peace, patience, kindness, goodness, faithfulness, gentleness, and self-control (Galatians 5:22–23).

Don't be afraid of the deaths God is calling you to. Trust that in His hands, every death leads to a resurrection. Every ending is a new beginning. Every surrender is a step closer to the abundant life Jesus promised us.

REFLECTION: Take some time to prayerfully consider what in your life needs to die so new life can spring forth. Is there a relationship that needs to be surrendered? A habit that needs to be laid down? A mindset that needs to be crucified? Ask God to give you the courage to die to these things, trusting in His power to bring resurrection and healing. Remember, in Christ we are continually being transformed into His image, "from glory to glory" (2 Corinthians 3:18 NKJV).

Day Twenty-Two

INNER TOOL CHEST

Let's talk about that **inner tool chest** of yours. You know, the one where you stash away all those painful emotions, memories, and problems that you don't want to deal with right now. It's like having a super-efficient, multi-drawer toolbox where you can tuck away anything that threatens your sense of control and well-being.

And you know what? It works. You can go about your day, focused on your tasks, relatively unaffected by those distracting feelings. You feel in command of your life, with everything neatly organized and under control.

But here's the thing. **That's not how God designed you to live.** In fact, those feelings of control and compartmentalization that you think are protecting you? They might actually be holding you back from experiencing the fullness of life that God has for you.

When you choose to live this way, it can be hard to access the emotions that enable you to connect deeply with others. **You might be harboring emotional wounds that are like ticking time bombs, waiting to explode when you least expect it.** You might struggle to be both a leader at work and emotionally present at home. Intimacy and emotionally charged situations might make you want to run for the hills.

But here's the good news. **Learning to live authentically means using your memories and feelings as tools to sculpt the life you want to live instead of storing them away and trying to function**

53

without them. Your experiences, your wounds, your emotions—they're all part of your story. They give your life texture and depth.

And when you turn them over to God? That's when the real transformation happens. Romans 8:28 says, "And we know that for those who love God all things work together for good, for those who are called according to his purpose." When you trust God with your weaknesses, He can use them for good. It's all part of your spiritual journey.

You don't have to have it all together. God wants to meet you right where you are, in the midst of your story with all of your messiness and your confusion and your unanswered questions and your pain. He wants to help you turn those wounds into wisdom, that brokenness into beauty. Trust Him with your story.

REFLECTION: Take some time to be honest with yourself. Journal about the memories, feelings, or wounds you've been compartmentalizing in an attempt to maintain control. Ask yourself: Do powerful emotions frighten me? Do I feel overwhelmed and threatened when engaged in close, intimate relationships or when confronted with painful memories?

WHAT EVERY SON NEEDS FROM DAD

As men, our relationship with our dad is one of the most significant influences in our story. Whether our dads were present or absent, loving or distant, their impact on our lives is profound. It shapes our sense of self, our confidence, our relationships with others, and even in some ways our understanding of God.

In reflecting on what a son needs from his dad, four essential elements stand out to me. These are some of the building blocks of a healthy, nurturing father-son relationship, the foundation on which a boy can grow into a secure, emotionally healthy man.

The first essential is time together. It's in the simple, everyday moments—a walk in the park, a shared project, going on trips together—that a son learns that he is valued, enjoyed, and loved. It's not just about the quantity of time but the quality. When a father chooses to invest his time and attention in his son, it sends a powerful message: "You matter to me. I delight in you."

A second essential is life skills. Ideally, a dad is his son's first and most important teacher. By equipping his son with practical skills—from changing a tire to managing finances to treating others with respect—a father gives his son the tools he needs to navigate life with confidence and competence.

A third essential is direction. A son needs his dad's wisdom and guidance as he figures out who he is and where he's headed. When a father shares his own journey, his values, and his faith, he provides his son with a compass for life's big questions.

But perhaps the most crucial essential is a father's heart. When a dad is emotionally present, when he's willing to be vulnerable and authentic, when he's generous with his affection and his words of affirmation, he gives his son an invaluable gift. He shows his son what it means to be a man of heart, a man who loves deeply and lives fully.

In Malachi 4:6, God speaks of the importance of this father-son heart connection, promising to "turn the hearts of fathers to their children and the hearts of children to their fathers." When a father opens his heart to his son, and a son feels safe to share his own heart with his father, something profound happens. The son learns to give and receive love, to trust, to be authentic. He sees a model of masculinity that is strong and tender, courageous and compassionate.

As you reflect on your own relationship with your dad, you may be able to experience gratefulness that you received these essentials from your dad, or you may recognize areas where these essentials were lacking. Perhaps your dad was physically or emotionally absent. Perhaps he was critical or harsh. Or maybe he simply didn't know how to express his love in the way you needed.

Acknowledging these wounds can be painful, but it's also a crucial step toward healing. When we have the courage to face our father wounds, to name them and bring them into the light, we open the door for God's grace to enter in.

The beautiful truth is, no matter what our earthly fathers may have lacked, we have a Heavenly Father who embodies these essentials perfectly. He is always present, always attentive, always eager to impart His wisdom. And His heart is fully, lavishly, unreservedly open to us. In Him, we find the affirmation, the direction, the unconditional love that our souls crave.

As you continue on your journey of authentic manhood, know that God wants to father you in all the ways you need. He wants to heal your father wounds, to fill the voids left by human imperfection. And He wants to equip you to be a man of heart, a man who can give generously to others from the abundance of love he's received.

Embrace your Heavenly Father today. Let Him show you the transforming power of a father's love. And watch as that love overflows into every area of your life, healing your past, anchoring your present, and shaping your future.

> **REFLECTION:** Take some time to honestly assess your relationship with your dad. In which of the four essential areas—time, life skills, direction, and heart—did he excel? In which areas did he struggle? How have these strengths and weaknesses shaped you? Bring your reflections to your Heavenly Father in prayer, asking Him to meet you in your areas of need and to father you with His perfect love.

Day Twenty-Four

UNLOCKING YOUR HEART

When you've experienced mistreatment, neglect, or abandonment from your mom, or if you've lived in fear of expressing your true needs and emotions, it's easy to grow into a man who denies himself a life of happiness, connection, and nurturing. You may find yourself locking your heart away, guarding it fiercely from further pain.

As you enter into manhood, the consequences of this emotional isolation begin showing up. Intimacy feels threatening, trust seems elusive, and identifying your own emotions becomes a daunting task. After years of suppressing your feelings, you may struggle to distinguish between genuine instincts and triggered responses.

God desires for you to live a life of freedom, wholeness, and authenticity. In John 10:10, Jesus declares, "I came that they may have life and have it abundantly." This abundant life is not one of emotional imprisonment but of liberation and healing.

The journey toward this freedom begins with self-awareness. It requires gently coaxing your heart out of hiding, acknowledging the pain and fear that have kept it locked away, not as a way of blaming but as a way of seeing. In Psalm 34:18, we're reminded that "the LORD is near to the brokenhearted and saves the crushed in spirit." Your Heavenly Father sees your wounded heart and longs to bring healing.

As you continue exploring your emotional world, extend to yourself the compassion and grace you may have been denied. As you do this you can learn to **honor your own emotions instead of burying them.**

59

Reflect on your childhood self not with judgment or disdain, but with empathy and understanding. **Recognize that this younger version of you was doing the best he could to navigate a challenging situation.** As you learn to embrace and comfort this part of yourself, you open the door to deeper self-acceptance and emotional and spiritual resilience.

This process of unlocking your heart is not one you should undertake alone. In fact, it's in the context of safe, supportive relationships that deep healing often occurs. As you grow in self-awareness and self-compassion, you may find yourself more willing to risk vulnerability with trusted others. Slowly, you can learn to let your guard down, to allow others to see and love the authentic you.

In 1 John 4:18, we're told that "perfect love casts out fear." As you experience the love of God and the love of safe, caring people, your fears will begin to dissipate. You'll find yourself more able to give and receive love, to experience the joy and peace that come from genuine connection.

Remember, **this journey of healing is both emotional and spiritual and it's not a linear one.** There will be setbacks and challenges along the way. But as you commit to the process, as you learn to extend grace to yourself and others, you'll find yourself stepping into the abundant life God has for you.

> **REFLECTION:** Take some time to reflect on your emotional world. Are there parts of your heart that remain locked away out of fear or self-protection? Consider writing a letter to your younger self, expressing the love, acceptance, and compassion you needed back then. As you go through your day, practice identifying your emotions as they arise, without judgment. When fear or self-criticism surface, counter them with truth from God's Word about your inherent worth and His unconditional love for you.

THE HEALING POWER OF A HEALTHY MARRIAGE

For the man who has chosen the path of marriage, a loving, committed relationship can be a powerful source of healing and growth. When a husband and wife create a bond built on honesty, vulnerability, and unconditional love, they form a safe haven where wounds can be tended to and authentic manhood can flourish.

In Ephesians 5:25, husbands are called to "love your wives, as Christ loved the church and gave himself up for her." **This kind of sacrificial, nurturing love creates an environment where both partners can let down their guards and be fully known and accepted.** For a man who has experienced the pain of past hurts, this unconditional love can be a healing balm, helping to counter lies he may have believed about his worth and lovability.

Of course, cultivating this kind of intimacy requires vulnerability and emotional risk-taking. It means being willing to share your story, your wounds, and your healing journey with your wife. This can be frightening for a man who has learned to equate vulnerability with weakness. **But when a man embraces the courage to open up to his wife, he invites her into a sacred space of connection and growth.**

Imagine the impact of having a life partner who knows your story, who has seen your scars, and who loves you all the more for them. A wife who cheers you on in your healing journey, who reminds

61

you of your worth when you doubt it, and who walks alongside you through every trial and triumph. This is the beauty and power of a healthy, Christ-centered marriage. **With Christ at the center of your marriage, you'll be continually reminded of the undeserving love and the unending grace He gives to both of you daily.**

This kind of relationship doesn't happen overnight. **It's built through countless small moments of choosing to seek Christ together, to be present with each other, to listen, to extend grace, and to ask for forgiveness.** It requires setting aside time for heartfelt conversations, for laughter, and for shared adventures. It means being intentional about creating a home life that is a refuge from the stresses and pressures of the world.

For the single man, this reflection is not meant to imply that marriage is a prerequisite for wholeness or healing. God's love and the support of a strong community can provide the acceptance and encouragement needed for growth. But for those who are married, embracing the potential for healing within your relationship can be a transformative part of your journey toward authentic manhood.

As you invite your wife into your story, you may find that your bond deepens in ways you never imagined. You may discover a new level of intimacy and partnership that brings joy and vitality to every area of your life. You may find that together, you can face any challenge and celebrate every victory.

REFLECTION: If you are married, take a moment to reflect on your relationship with your wife. How have you experienced healing and growth through your bond? Are there areas where you could be more open and vulnerable with her? Consider expressing your gratitude to your wife for her role in your life and discussing how you can continue to cultivate authentic connection. If you are single, reflect on the relationships in your life that provide support and encouragement. How can you continue to build a community that fosters your growth and wholeness?

Day Twenty-Six

FIXING OUR EYES ON JESUS

In a world full of distractions and competing voices, it's easy for us to lose sight of what authentic manhood really looks like. We can find ourselves chasing after success, status, or approval, only to end up feeling empty and unfulfilled. But amid all the noise, there is one voice that calls out to us, inviting us to a different way of living. It's the voice of Jesus, our ultimate mentor and model.

Hebrews 12:2 encourages us to keep "looking to Jesus, the founder and perfecter of our faith." When we look to Jesus, we see a man who fully embraced His humanity while also embodying the divine. He showed us what it looks like to live a life of compassion, integrity, and self-sacrificial love.

Jesus tells us in John 10:9, "I am the door. If anyone enters by me, he will be saved and will go in and out and find pasture." He calls Himself the door we are to walk through. **When we walk through Him, we find the abundant life He promised. We discover the pastures of purpose, meaning, and deep soul satisfaction.**

But walking with Jesus doesn't mean life will always be easy. Remember, He told His disciples that in this world we would face our fair share of troubles (John 16:33). As men living out of broken, wounded, and selfish hearts, we will face challenges, setbacks, and disappointments. There will be times when that little negative voice in our head tells us we're not good enough, that we don't measure up.

In those moments, it's crucial that we don't lose heart. That we don't lose focus. That we keep our eyes fixed on Jesus, the author and finisher of our faith.

Remember Peter walking on the water? As long as he kept his gaze on Jesus, he was able to do the impossible. But the moment he looked away, the moment he let the wind and the waves distract him, he began to sink (Matthew 14:22–33). The same is true for us. **When we keep our eyes on Jesus, we can walk through the storms of life with a steady heart and a sure foot.** But when we look away, we can quickly find ourselves sinking.

So how do you practically fix your eyes on Jesus? **It means choosing daily to spend time in His presence, reading His Word, and communing with Him in prayer.** It means surrounding yourself with a community of believers who can encourage you and point you back to Christ. It means regularly reflecting on His life and teachings, asking yourself, "What would Jesus do in this situation?"

As we do this, as we keep Jesus as our North Star, we'll find that His life becomes the lens through which we see everything else. Our definition of success, of significance, of manhood itself will be transformed. We'll find ourselves less driven by the fleeting approval of others and more anchored in the unshakable love and acceptance of Christ.

This is the heart of authentic manhood—not a perfectionism that leaves us constantly striving and constantly falling short but a humble dependence on the perfect One. A recognition that in our weakness, His strength is made perfect (2 Corinthians 12:9).

So today, if you find yourself feeling lost, discouraged, or distracted, refix your eyes on Jesus. Look to Him as your mentor, your model, your source of hope and guidance. And trust that as you walk with Him and through Him, He will lead you into the abundant life He destined you for.

> **REFLECTION:** Consider where you've been looking for direction and validation. Have you been more focused on the approval of others or the standards of the world than on following Jesus? Take a moment to reorient your heart and mind. Ask God to help you keep your eyes fixed on Him, no matter what storms may come your way.

Day Twenty-Seven

THE HEALING POWER OF HONEST SHARING

None of us have it all together, we all carry wounds and scars—many of them stemming from our relationships, oftentimes from mom and dad. Even those of us blessed with loving, present, and caring moms and dads were not raised by perfect people. They, too, carried their own wounds and struggles, which inevitably affected us in some way.

When we hear others share honestly about their own wounds, it can be a profound source of healing for us. Proverbs 27:17 reminds us that iron sharpens iron. Their vulnerability and authenticity can give us the courage to acknowledge our own pain, to see our own stories in a new light.

There's power in speaking our truths out loud, in giving voice to the hurts we've carried silently for so long. When we share our stories with trusted others, we invite them to bear witness to our pain, to stand with us in solidarity and support, and we experience the freedom of being real.

When we put ourselves in settings and situations that foster this kind of openness, we give a gift to ourselves and to those around us. We create space for healing, for growth, for genuine connection.

Seek out these kinds of moments. Look for opportunities to share your story with people who have earned your trust, who will honor your experiences and support you in your healing. And be

67

ready to offer the same kind of presence and compassion to others as they share their own stories.

Be reminded that God is the Father of compassion who comforts us in all our troubles, so that we can then offer comfort to others who are hurting (2 Corinthians 1:3–4). As we open up to others and to God, we find the healing and strength we need to move forward.

REFLECTION: Think about a time when you experienced the power of honest sharing. What was it about that experience that made it feel safe and transformative? How might you cultivate more of these moments in your life?

MY EMOTIONAL HUNGER

You know that feeling when you're getting hungry, and dinner is still hours away? You can ignore it for a while, but sooner or later, you need to eat.

You have an emotional hunger too. It's that inner place of need that's longing to be satisfied. And sometimes, it's hard to tell whether those hunger pangs are coming from a physical need or a deeper emotional one.

It's easy to mistake emotional longing for physical hunger. That's why some guys turn to overeating or even binge eating, trying to quiet that latent emotional hunger. But let me tell you, pretending you don't need closeness, intimacy, or companionship? That's only going to make you more hungry.

It's good to remind yourself daily God didn't create you to be entirely self-sufficient. The apostle Paul tells us that it is the will of Christ for us to carry each other's burdens (Galatians 6:2). We were made to support one another, to share in each other's joys and sorrows, to do life together.

So what do we do with that gnawing emotional hunger? Acknowledge it. Fully taste what life has to offer. Risk the kind of openness and receptiveness necessary for the caring, nurturing, and love that we've often fearfully rejected.

And you know what? God gets it. He equates eternal life with an abundant feast made complete with many peoples. Look at Isaiah

25:6: "On this mountain the LORD of hosts will make for all peoples a feast of rich food, a feast of well-aged wine, of rich food full of marrow, of aged wine well refined."

Your emotional needs are valid. God gave them to you for a reason. **He wants to satisfy that hunger with His love and with the love of others.** Don't be afraid to acknowledge your longing and take steps to nourish your soul, to be loved, to be known, and to be fulfilled.

> **REFLECTION:** Take a moment to reflect on these questions: Do you attempt to ignore your feelings of loneliness and your longing for love? Do you often try to tough it out, ignoring your inner needs or labeling them as "weak"? What kind of life are you hungering for in your heart and soul? Why do you sometimes feel you don't deserve to be loved? How can you begin to open your heart compassionately to yourself, to God, and to others?

Day Twenty-Nine

BREAKING THE CYCLE OF CRITICISM

If you grew up with a critical father, the echoes of his disapproval more than likely reverberate into your psyche long into adulthood. The words that were spoken (or left unspoken) in your childhood have a way of etching themselves into your soul, shaping the way you see yourself and others.

Proverbs 18:21 reminds us that "death and life are in the power of the tongue." **When a father's tongue is a weapon of criticism, it can wound a child's sense of self-worth, leaving scars that are carried into future relationships.**

If you've internalized your father's harsh critiques, which is more than probable, you may find yourself perpetuating the cycle, becoming your own harshest critic and holding others to an impossible standard. You may struggle with anger, lashing out at those closest to you and then drowning in waves of guilt and shame. This pattern of "rage, rinse, repeat" can feel like an inescapable inheritance.

But there is hope for breaking free. Remember what we're told in 2 Corinthians 5:17. It says, "Therefore, if anyone is in Christ, he is a new creation. The old has passed away; behold, the new has come." **In Christ, you are not defined by your father's words or actions but by your identity as a beloved child of God.**

Embracing this truth is a journey of courage and grace. It requires looking at your father with adult eyes, recognizing that his criticism was a reflection of his own pain and not a measure of your worth. It means choosing to forgive him, not excusing the hurt but releasing its hold on your heart.

As you do this hard work, you'll begin to discover your own unique characteristics, your God-given strengths and purpose. You'll begin learning to define yourself not by the echoes of the past but by the truth of who you are in Christ. This is the path to authentic manhood—a path marked by freedom, self-acceptance, and the courage to live out your own mission.

Galatians 5:1 declares, "It is for freedom that Christ has set us free. Stand firm, then, and do not let yourselves be burdened again by a yoke of slavery" (NIV). When we break the cycle of criticism and step into our true identity, we experience this freedom. We are no longer slaves to our father's approval or disapproval but free to live the abundant life Christ has for us.

Remember, you don't have to be defined by your past but by the love of your Heavenly Father. Embrace your true identity and step into the freedom and purpose He has for you.

> **REFLECTION:** Reflect on your relationship with your father. Did you experience a critical or disapproving father? How have those experiences shaped the way you see yourself and others? Take a moment to bring those wounds to your Heavenly Father. Ask Him to show you the truth of your identity in Christ. Surround yourself with friends and mentors who affirm your unique strengths and purpose. Choose to break the cycle of criticism by extending grace— to your father, to others, and to yourself.

HEALTHY BOUNDARIES

As you reflect on your relationship with mom, you might recognize a pattern of emotional swaddling. Perhaps your mom, while well-intentioned, struggled to let go of her control over your life. She may have doted on you, made decisions for you, and crossed boundaries in a way that left you feeling stifled and unable to fully mature into your own person.

Scripture highlights the importance of a healthy separation from your parents in order to form a strong, united bond with your wife. Genesis 2:24 says, "Therefore a man shall leave his father and his mother and hold fast to his wife, and they shall become one flesh." This doesn't mean abandoning your parents but rather establishing a new primary relationship.

If you find yourself caught in a tug-of-war between your mom's expectations and your own adult life, you're not alone. Many men struggle to navigate this delicate balance, wanting to honor their mom while also establishing their independence. But when moms fail to make a healthy break with their adult sons, it can lead to tension and frustration for everyone involved.

Jesus affirms the sanctity of the marriage bond in Matthew 19:6, saying, "So they are no longer two but one flesh. What therefore God has joined together, let not man separate." Allowing your mom's influence to interfere with your marriage could very well invite division into a relationship intended by God to be unified.

Breaking free from emotional swaddling requires courage and assertiveness. It means learning to kindly but firmly communicate your boundaries with your mom, even if it feels uncomfortable at first. Proverbs 25:28 warns, "A man without self-control is like a city broken into and left without walls." By exercising self-control and setting healthy limits, you protect your personal well-being and the integrity of your relationships.

Remember, **establishing boundaries is not about rejecting your mom or disregarding her feelings**. Rather, it's about maturing into the man God created you to be—**a man who can love and honor his mom while also leading his own life**. Trust in God's guidance and grace to help you find the right balance.

> **REFLECTION:** Take some time to prayerfully consider the dynamics between you and your mom. Are there areas where you need to establish clearer boundaries? Do you struggle with assertiveness or conflict avoidance that is keeping you from saying what needs to be said? Pray for courage and clarity as you consider the need for kind but firm communication with your mom.

Day Thirty-One

LISTENING TO THE STORIES OUR BODIES ARE TELLING US

Our bodies are incredible storytellers. They hold the narratives of our joys and sorrows, our triumphs and traumas. **When we learn to listen to the messages our bodies are sending us, we gain valuable insights into our emotional and spiritual well-being.**

The apostle Paul recognized this deep connection between body and spirit when he wrote in 1 Corinthians 6:19–20, "Or do you not know that your body is a temple of the Holy Spirit within you, whom you have from God? You are not your own, for you were bought with a price. So glorify God in your body."

For many of us, our bodies give us clues about our emotional and spiritual well-being. Stress, for example, can manifest in a variety of physical symptoms—headaches, muscle tension, digestive issues, and more. Unresolved emotional pain can contribute to chronic pain, fatigue, and a weakened immune system. **Our bodies bear the weight of the stories we carry.**

As you come to understand your story more fully and to heal holistically, you must listen to your body. I've learned in my own personal story how unhealthy stress, a lazy diet, and inadequate exercise went straight to my heart in my early adult years, despite my history as a college athlete and very active person. I had to humble myself, listen to what my hurting heart was telling me, and change my ways as I learned to deal with stress in healthy ways, eat healthier, and make high-intensity workouts part of my daily routine.

I also experienced a season in life when I was letting fear grip my soul after the unexpected death of my younger brother. It expressed itself in unwanted panic attacks in the middle of the night. My body was telling me to let go and to trust God. **It was telling me to sit with Jesus in my fears and to learn to just breathe with Him, to breathe in His goodness and His love, and to breathe out my fears instead of letting them build up inside.** I've learned firsthand that our body is a real part of our emotional and spiritual healthiness.

So as you pursue healing in your heart and mind, it's crucial that you also attend to the healing of your body.

- Practice mindfulness and body awareness, noticing physical sensations without judgment

- Engage in regular physical activity and exercise that builds strength and endurance and releases endorphins

- Prioritize rest and sleep, giving your body the downtime it needs to heal and recharge

- Nourish your body with wholesome, nutritious foods

- Seek medical care when needed, and be honest with health care providers about emotional factors that may be affecting physical health

As noted author and psychiatrist Bessel A. van der Kolk wisely notes, **"The body keeps score . . . In order to change, people need to become aware of their sensations and the way that their bodies interact with the world around them. Physical self-awareness is the first step in releasing the tyranny of the past."**[1]

---

1. Van Der Kolk, *Bessel A. The Body Keeps the Score: Brain, Mind, and Body in the Healing of Trauma.* Penguin Books, 2015.

By tuning into the stories our bodies are telling us, we gain a more holistic picture of our well-being. We can begin to identify patterns and triggers and make choices that support healing on every level—physical, emotional, and spiritual.

This process of body awareness is a journey, not a destination. It requires patience, curiosity, and self-compassion. There will be days when we feel strong and vibrant, and days when our bodies are asking for extra care and kindness. Through it all, we can trust that God is with us, working toward our wholeness and flourishing.

REFLECTION: Take a moment to do a body scan, bringing awareness to any physical sensations you're experiencing. Are there areas of tension, discomfort, or ease? Consider how your emotional state may be affecting your physical well-being. What changes do you need to make today to better take care your body and listen to the stories it's telling? Remember, your body is a gift, a sacred vessel deserving of your care and respect and is a big part of your personal story.

Day Thirty-Two

REST AND RESTORATION

Life has a way of beating us down. As men, we often feel the weight of responsibility, the pressure to perform, to provide, to be strong. We carry the burdens of our work, our families, our own expectations. And over time, these burdens can leave us feeling worn out, discouraged, and even hopeless. If this is where we stay for too long, the negative impact on our life story can be significant and leave us with more regret than abundance.

In these moments, where do you turn for refreshment? For rest? For renewal?

The world offers us many escapes—entertainment, substances, workaholism. But these are temporary balms, mere Band-Aids on a deeper wound. They may numb the pain for a moment, but they don't provide true healing.

There is only one place where we can consistently find the deep soul rest we crave. It's in the loving, grace-filled arms of Jesus.

Jesus Himself understood the need for this kind of rest. Throughout the Gospels, we see Him withdrawing from the crowds, taking time to be alone with His Heavenly Father. In Mark 6:31, He invites His disciples to do the same: "And he said to them, 'Come away by yourselves to a desolate place and rest a while.'"

This is an invitation He extends to us as well. In Matthew 11:28–30, Jesus says, **"Come to me, all who labor and are heavy laden, and I will give you rest. Take my yoke upon you, and learn from me, for**

I am gentle and lowly in heart, and you will find rest for your souls. For my yoke is easy and my burden is light."

When we come to Jesus, we can lay down our burdens. We can hand over our stress, our worries, our guilt, and our shame. We can trust that He will carry these things for us, that His yoke is easy and His burden is light.

This doesn't mean that all our problems disappear. But it does mean that we don't have to carry them alone. We have a Savior who is ready and willing to bear them with us and for us.

Finding rest in Jesus also means taking time to simply be with Him. To quiet your mind, to unclutter your thoughts, to let go of all the things you're holding so tightly. It's in these moments of stillness that you can hear His voice more clearly, that you can receive His love and grace more deeply.

This type of rest and reflection is a crucial part of your journey toward authentic manhood. It's how you recalibrate, how you remember who you are and Whose you are. It's how you gain perspective on what truly matters.

So today, if you're feeling weary, worn out, or overwhelmed, accept Jesus's invitation. Take a moment to come to Him, to lay your burdens down, to receive His rest. Trust that in His presence, you will find the refreshment and renewal your soul craves.

Remember, you are not defined solely by your productivity or your performance. You are defined by your identity as a beloved child of God. And it's from that place of belovedness that you can live out your unique, meaningful story—not perfectly, but faithfully, as a man made in God's image.

REFLECTION: What burdens are you carrying that you need to lay down at Jesus's feet? What would it look like for you to carve out time each day to simply be with Him, to rest in His presence? How might regular times of rest and reflection affect your journey toward authentic manhood?

SEEING YOUR STORY CLEARLY

It's normal to feel a deep desire to be proud of our parents, to hold them up as the heroes and protectors we long for them to be. That's a normal thing to feel. But this desire can lead us into a trap of selective vision, where we unconsciously distort our memories and perceptions to fit the narrative we want to believe. We may minimize the impact of their brokenness, their wounds, and their mistakes, in an attempt to protect ourselves from the pain of acknowledging the ways they've fallen short.

It's crucial that you're honest with yourself as you view your own story and your relationships. It's also important to distinguish between speaking truth and bashing our parents. The goal is not to judge or condemn them, but rather to see them clearly, as the flawed and human individuals they are.

When we're able to acknowledge the reality of our parents' brokenness and how it has affected us, we open the door for genuine healing and growth. Psalm 34:18 assures us, "The LORD is near to the brokenhearted and saves the crushed in spirit." God wants to meet us in the truth of our stories, to bring His healing and redemption to the wounds we've carried.

This process of seeing clearly is not about dwelling on the past or wallowing in blame. Rather, it's about giving ourselves permission to grieve what we didn't receive, to validate our own

experiences and emotions. In doing so, we create space for Jesus to enter into our pain, to bring His comfort and His transforming grace.

It's natural to want to take responsibility for the relationships that have shaped us, to believe that if we had just been better, smarter, or more worthy, things would have been different. But the truth is, our parents' choices and actions were their own.

Letting go of this misplaced responsibility is a crucial step in our healing. It allows us to extend grace to our parents, to see them as the broken individuals they are without excusing or minimizing the impact of their actions. It also frees us to embrace our own stories, to trust in the validity of our experiences and emotions.

As you continue on your journey of growth and healing, be gentle with yourself. Seeing your story clearly is a process, one that often requires the support and perspective of trusted others. Seek out safe spaces and relationships where you can share your experiences and receive validation and encouragement.

Remember, your story, with all its joys and sorrows, has shaped you into the man you are today. As you learn to see it clearly, you open yourself up to the healing and redemptive work God wants to do in and through you.

> **REFLECTION:** Are there areas where you've engaged in selective vision, minimizing the impact of others' brokenness in an attempt to protect yourself or them? Ask God to give you the courage to see your story clearly and the wisdom to know how to process and integrate these truths in a healthy way. Remember, this is not about bashing or blaming but about creating space for healing and growth.

FACING THE TIGER

In the face of emotional vulnerability, our instincts often scream at us to run. When the prospect of intimacy triggers our deepest fears and insecurities, it can feel like staring down a hungry tiger. Every fiber of our being wants to turn and flee, to retreat to the safety of isolation.

But as authentic men, we are called to a different response. We are called to stand firm, to face our fears head-on, and to trust in the One who is always with us.

In Joshua 1:9, God commands Joshua to "be strong and courageous. Do not be frightened, and do not be dismayed, for the LORD your God is with you wherever you go." God knew that Joshua would face many "tigers" as he led the Israelites into the Promised Land. But He also knew that Joshua's strength and courage would come from His presence.

The same is true for us. When we face the tigers of emotional vulnerability, we don't do so alone. We have the power of Christ within us, the same power that raised Jesus from the dead (Ephesians 1:19–20). This is the source of our internal strength—not our own willpower or determination but our intimate, dependent relationship with Jesus.

It's in this relationship that we find the grace to stand our ground when every instinct tells us to run. It's in His love that we find the security to open our hearts, even when it feels risky. And it's in His strength that we find the courage to pursue authentic connection, even when it's uncomfortable.

This doesn't mean that facing our fears becomes easy. It doesn't mean that we won't feel the panic rise in our throats or the adrenaline surge through our veins. But it does mean that in the midst of these feelings, we have an anchor. We have a safe harbor. We have a God who whispers to our racing hearts, "Peace, be still" (Mark 4:39 NKJV).

In these moments, we can engage in a different kind of self-talk. Instead of giving in to the voice of fear, we can speak the truth of God's Word over ourselves:

- "When I am afraid, I put my trust in you." (Psalm 56:3)

- "I can do all things through him who strengthens me." (Philippians 4:13)

- "For God gave us a spirit not of fear but of power and love and self-control." (2 Timothy 1:7)

These are the promises we cling to as we face our fears. These are the truths that enable us to stand firm, to look our fears in the eye, and to step into the risky, rewarding work of authentic connection.

And as we do this, as we refuse to run from intimacy, we find that on the other side of our fear is a richer, more meaningful life. We discover the joy of being fully known and fully loved. We experience the depth of connection that God designed us for.

So if you find yourself facing a tiger today—whether it's the vulnerability of a difficult conversation, the risk of opening up to a friend, or the fear of letting your guard down with your spouse—remember that you are not alone. Remember that the same God who faced down death itself is with you, within you, ready to empower you with His strength.

Lean into Him. Trust in Him. And watch as He transforms your fear into faith, your isolation into intimacy, and your timidity into a courageous, abundant life.

> **REFLECTION:** What tigers of emotional vulnerability are you facing right now? How can you lean into God's strength and presence as you face these fears? Take a moment to bring your specific fears to God in prayer, asking Him to fill you with His peace, His courage, and His love.

FROM EARTHLY WOUNDS TO HEAVENLY HEALING

As men who have experienced wounding in our lives, we often find ourselves building emotional barriers to protect our hearts from further wounding. Like a science fiction force field, these invisible walls serve as a defense mechanism, keeping others at a safe distance. We may appear to desire closeness, but those who attempt to draw near inevitably collide with our well-fortified boundaries.

At the core of these barriers often lies a festering father wound—a deep hurt inflicted by an imperfect earthly father. Whether through absence, criticism, or lack of affection, these wounds can shape your sense of self-worth and your ability to trust others.

But our Heavenly Father is not content to leave us trapped behind these walls of pain. He is a God of healing, a God who desires to walk with us through the valleys of life. As Psalm 147:3 declares, "He heals the brokenhearted and binds up their wounds."

When you take your father wounds to God, you open yourself to a love that transcends human limitations. **You encounter a Heavenly Father who is consistently present, unconditionally accepting, and abundantly gracious.** In His presence, your wounded heart finds the validation, comfort, and healing it so desperately needs.

This journey of healing also involves extending forgiveness to your imperfect earthly father. Ephesians 4:32 instructs us to "Be

87

kind to one another, tenderhearted, forgiving one another, as God in Christ forgave you." When we choose to forgive, we release ourselves from the burden of bitterness and resentment. We step into the freedom that allows us to embrace our true, authentic selves—the men God created us to be.

Forgiveness doesn't mean excusing hurtful behaviors or neglecting healthy boundaries. Rather, it is a decision to relinquish our right to revenge, to entrust justice to God, and to extend the same grace that we so desperately need ourselves. As we do this difficult but crucial work, we experience the healing power of forgiveness firsthand.

The path to wholeness is not always easy, but we do not walk it alone. Our Heavenly Father is with us every step of the way, ready to bind up our wounds and lead us into the abundant life He has for us.

> **REFLECTION:** Take a moment to reflect on the emotional barriers you may have built due to your father wound. Consider bringing these hurts to your Heavenly Father in prayer, asking Him to begin the process of healing in your heart. If you harbor bitterness toward your earthly father, pray for the strength to forgive, remembering the forgiveness you have received in Christ. Trust that as you take these steps, God will meet you with His transformative love and grace.

UNTANGLING THE APRON STRINGS

Picture this: You're a grown man, perhaps married with kids of your own. But every time you make a decision, big or small, you find yourself running it by your mom first. She's always been your go-to for advice, approval, and emotional support. **While it's great to have a close relationship with your mom, there comes a point where you need to get untangled from the apron strings and stand on your own two feet.**

Remember, a man shall leave his father and his mother and hold fast to his wife, and they shall become one flesh. This verse emphasizes the importance of creating a new family unit, with your spouse as your primary partner and confidant.

But what does this look like in day-to-day life? It might mean making decisions with your wife without feeling the need to consult your mom first. It could involve setting boundaries around how often you call or visit your mom, ensuring that your spouse and children are your top priorities. It definitely means learning to rely on God and your own judgment rather than defaulting to your mom's opinion on every matter.

Of course, this isn't always easy, especially if your mom has been a central figure in your life. She may feel hurt or rejected as you start to pull away and establish your independence. That's where clear, loving communication comes in. Explain to your mom that while you cherish your relationship with her, you also need to focus on your own family and personal growth.

Ephesians 4:15 encourages us to speak the truth in love, which is key when navigating these sensitive conversations. You can honor your mother while still setting healthy boundaries. This might sound like, "Mom, I appreciate your advice, but I need to make this decision with my wife," or "I know you love having me visit, but I also need to prioritize time with my own family."

Untangling the apron strings is a process, but it's a crucial one for your maturity and the health of your marriage. As you take steps to establish your independence, remember that your ultimate dependence should be on God. Lean into His guidance and strength as you navigate this area of your life.

REFLECTION: Consider the practical areas of your life where you might be overly reliant on your mom. Is it in decision-making? Emotional support? Approval seeking? Identify one concrete step you can take this week to untangle the apron strings in that area, whether it's making a decision without consulting your mom or carving out quality time with your spouse. Pray for wisdom, courage, and grace as you begin to establish a healthier, more independent relationship with your mom.

THE HEALED MAN

Hopefully by this point in your story and in spending time in these daily reflections, you've identified and owned some of your emotional wounds. As I've said, we all carry wounds. And just like a physical injury, if our emotional and spiritual wounds are left untreated, they can fester, infecting every aspect of our lives and relationships. The resulting sickness can cause significant harm to ourselves and those around us—our marriages, our families, our communities.

Through the power of Christ, you can experience deep, transformative healing from your wounds. You can move from a place of brokenness to a place of wholeness. The journey isn't always easy, but it's one that leads to a more abundant, authentic life.

Consider the difference between a man who hasn't experienced healing and one who has.

The man who has not healed:

- is often unable to fully live in the present. Part of his soul remains rooted in his past, tethered to the pain and trauma he's experienced. He may find himself constantly reliving old hurts, unable to move forward.

- is often easily angered. His wounds sit just beneath the surface, raw and ready to be triggered. This anger can spill over onto others who aren't the real cause or source of his pain, damaging relationships and pushing people away.

- may find forgiveness to be a struggle. Even if he sincerely wants to forgive those who have hurt him, he may find himself unable to truly let go, his wounds keeping him chained to bitterness and resentment.

- may struggle with self-worth. He may question his value, blaming himself for conflicts or failures that may have had little to do with him. His identity is shaken, uncertain.

The man who has healed:

- can be at peace with his past. He's able to acknowledge the wounds he's carried without being defined by them. This freedom allows him to fully engage with the present and move boldly into the future God has for him.

- is no longer controlled by his anger. He may still experience righteous anger at injustice or wrongdoing, but it's a measured, appropriate response rather than an uncontrolled reaction.

- recognizes that forgiveness is possible. He's able to extend the same grace and compassion that Christ has extended to him. This forgiveness doesn't erase the wrong that was done, but it frees him from the burden of unforgiveness.

- his self-worth is in an unshakable place—his identity as a beloved son of God. He knows that he was created, rescued, and valued by a Father who will never fail or abandon him. This knowledge anchors him, giving him a confidence that isn't dependent on his performance or others' opinions.

Healing is a journey—a journey worth taking. **As you allow God to bind up your wounds, to mend your brokenness, you will find yourself more able to love more deeply, to forgive more freely, to pursue your God-given callings with more confidence and purpose.**

So if you find yourself carrying wounds today, don't lose heart. The Healer is here, ready to meet you in your pain and lead you into wholeness. Take a step toward Him today, trusting in His power to restore and renew.

REFLECTION: As you compare and contrast the differences between a healed man and an unhealed man, how might healing your wounds change the way you engage with the present and move into the future? What's one step you can take today to invite God into your journey of healing?

CULTIVATING CONNECTION THROUGH HEALING

As you navigate your relationships, it's important to recognize the difference between *bonding* and *binding*. When you carry unhealed wounds, it's easy to fall into patterns of **binding**—attempting to control your relationships out of fear and insecurity. But true connection, the kind that fosters joy, love, and mutual commitment, requires a different approach.

When we engage in bonding rather than binding, we create space for supportive, life-giving connection. In order to cultivate these bonded relationships, we must all first do the work of self-awareness and healing. This means taking an honest look at your own fears and insecurities, the wounds that drive you to cling too tightly or keep others at a distance. It means acknowledging the ways you've sought to control your relationships rather than allowing for genuine emotional, spiritual, and physical intimacy.

As you begin to understand and address your own wounds, you create space for a new kind of relationship—one built on trust, vulnerability, grace, and mutual care. It's built on the kind of love mentioned in 1 John 4:18, a love that casts out fear.

Imagine the impact this kind of bonded love could have on your marriage, your parenting, your friendships, and even your

work relationships. When you let go of the need to control and instead open yourself up to authentic connection, you invite others to do the same. You create an environment where love can flourish, where each person feels seen, heard, and valued for who they are.

Of course, this process of letting go and learning to bond is not a one-time event. It's a daily choice, a continual practice of turning toward connection rather than control. It requires patience and grace, both with yourself and with others. It means extending grace when fears and old patterns resurface, while remaining committed to the healing journey.

As you engage in this important work, lean into God's love and His grace. Allow it to be your foundation as you learn to love others more deeply and show grace more freely.

REFLECTION: Take a moment to consider your own relationships. Are there areas where you've found yourself binding rather than bonding? What fears or insecurities might be driving these patterns? Bring these to God in prayer, asking for His wisdom and strength as you begin the work of healing and cultivating healthier connections.

SURRENDERING THE FLAG

Have you ever approached relationships like you're trying to win a war? You know, always striving to maintain power, claim your turf, and come out on top? I get it. But let me tell you, that approach doesn't usually lead to happy endings when it comes to the people we care about.

Sometimes, we need to surrender the flag in order to find common ground. And often, that urge to control everything and everyone around us? It's rooted in feeling out of control somewhere in our past.

So take a moment to look back. Keep unpacking and examining how those past battles are shaping who you are today. You can't go back and win those lost fights from yesterday. But you can look back to understand how they're affecting your behavior right now.

When you take the time to reflect on your past, you might see a younger version of yourself that felt the need to create personal fallout shelters to protect your heart. Or maybe you'd see a kid suiting up in armor, ready to fight tooth and nail to win, no matter the cost. And if you're honest, you might realize that you're still battling through life with that same mentality, always on high alert, viewing everyone as a potential enemy.

We can't rewrite our history, whether it's filled with joy or pain. But we can change the way we see it. We can't live a different story than our own. But we can decide how the next chapter unfolds. As the apostle Paul writes in Philippians 3:13–14, "Brothers and sisters, I do not consider myself yet to have taken hold of it. But one thing I do: Forgetting what is behind and straining toward what is ahead, I press on toward the goal to win the prize for which God has called me heavenward in Christ Jesus" (NIV).

It's only when we lay down our weapons and step back from the fight that we can begin to see things more clearly. And when we start to understand the impact of our past on our present, that's when we can stop battling and start truly living.

Remember, looking back isn't about dwelling on the past. It's about understanding how it's shaped you so that you can move forward with wisdom, grace, and a renewed sense of purpose. God wants to help you write a story of redemption, healing, and hope. Trust Him to guide you as you lay down your flag, leave behind what needs to be left behind, and press on toward the goal He has for you.

> **REFLECTION:** Do you react with defensiveness, anger, or annoyance when your spouse or partner asks something of you? Do you often perceive others' comments as criticisms? Are you always on high alert, waiting for the next shoe to drop? How can you begin to lay down your weapons and start writing a new chapter in your story?

Day Forty

DIFFUSING THE PRESSURE WITHIN

As wounded men, we often find ourselves bottling up our feelings, sealing them away from the world and even from ourselves. We tuck away the hurt, the anger, the pain, thinking that if we don't acknowledge these emotions, they will simply disappear. But the truth is, these unaddressed feelings are boiling below the surface, waiting for the slightest provocation to explode.

When we fail to process our emotions in a healthy way, we create a pressurized potential within ourselves. One wrong move, one trigger, and suddenly, we erupt, spewing our pent-up pain onto those around us. Like shards of glass from a shattered bottle, our words and actions can wound the very people we love and care about.

Oftentimes with men, at the root of this bottled-up anger lies a deep father wound. Any unresolved hurt from a father who was absent, critical, or abusive can fester within us, coloring our interactions and reactions. But how do we diffuse this pressurized potential? How do we release our anger and pain in ways that bring healing rather than harm?

One important key to releasing our anger and pain in ways that bring healing lies in examining the "messages" we carry within. Each painful memory, each unresolved hurt, is like a message in a bottle—a distress signal from our past self. By taking the time to carefully extract and read these messages, one by one, we begin

99

to diffuse the pressure. We acknowledge the pain, the fear, the long-ing—and in doing so, we create space for healing.

This process of self-examination is not easy, but you do not un-dertake it alone. Jesus, our ever-present Savior, desires to meet you in the deep, dark places you fear to tread. **He offers a beautiful invita-tion to us in Matthew 11:28–30 when He says, "Come to me, all who labor and are heavy laden, and I will give you rest. Take my yoke upon you, and learn from me, for I am gentle and lowly in heart, and you will find rest for your souls. For my yoke is easy, and my burden is light."**

When we invite Jesus into our bottled-up emotions, He can take our shattered pieces and create a mosaic of grace. He can redeem your pain, using it to shape you into a man of compassion, wisdom, and strength. As 2 Corinthians 4:7 reminds us, "We have this treasure in jars of clay to show that this all-surpassing power is from God and not from us" (NIV).

REFLECTION: Set aside time to examine the messages you've bottled up inside. Choose one memory or emotion to focus on and bring it before Jesus in prayer. Ask Him to meet you in that place of pain, to bring His healing touch. As you process these emotions, consider how releasing them might affect your relationships with others.

GROWING INTO YOUR OWN SHOES

You may have fond memories of, as a young boy, slipping your small feet into your dad's big shoes, feeling a sense of pride, power, and identity. It's a common boyhood experience, a playful moment of trying on the role of the man of the house.

However, for some boys, particularly those with absent fathers, this symbolic act can take on a more serious meaning. You might have found yourself stepping into your dad's shoes too soon, taking on emotional responsibilities that were beyond your years. Perhaps you felt a need to protect and care for your mom, to fill the void left by your father's absence. While your intentions were undoubtedly noble, this premature thrust into adulthood could have long-lasting effects.

Scripture reminds us in 1 Corinthians 13:11, "When I was a child, I spoke like a child, I thought like a child, I reasoned like a child. When I became a man, I gave up childish ways." There's a natural progression to growing up, a time and season for each stage of development. **When that process is disrupted, it can affect your sense of identity and your relationships in adulthood.**

If you find yourself still feeling responsible for your mom's wellbeing, even at the expense of your own relationships and needs, it may be time to reflect on this dynamic. **While it's commendable to care for others, especially your own mom, it's essential to recog-**

nize the limits of your responsibility and not do it in a way that causes lack of attention and resentment in your own home with your own family.

If you're a married man your primary focus should be on loving and leading your wife and family well. Ephesians 5:25 reminds us to love our wife "as Christ loved the church and gave himself up for her." This sacrificial love requires emotional investment and energy. **If you find yourself stretched thin trying to meet mom's unreasonable expectations for support and relational connection, it can strain your ability to fully show up for your spouse and children.**

It's important to find a healthy balance, one that honors your mom while also prioritizing your God-given role as a husband and father. As I've said before, you may really need to set gentle boundaries, communicating your limitations, and helping your mom seek additional sources of support and connection. Remember, you are not responsible for filling every emotional need in your mom's life, especially at the cost of your own family's well-being.

Be mindful and prayerful of navigating this balance well. Proverbs 11:14 reminds us that there is safety in an abundance of counselors. If you're feeling stuck in this, get some new perspectives and opinions from others you trust and who have maybe even navigated this journey with their own family.

Ultimately, trust that as you seek to honor God in your relationships, He will give you the grace and guidance you need. Lean into His love and strength, knowing that He knows your heart to honor your mom and love your wife well.

> **REFLECTION:** Take a moment to consider how you're balancing your role as a husband and father with the expectations placed on you by your mom. Are there areas where you need to establish healthier boundaries or communicate more clearly? How can you prioritize your marriage and family while still showing love and respect to your mom?

SCARS AND STORIES

Every scar tells a story. Each mark on our bodies is a reminder of a past wound, a moment of pain or trauma that has left its indelible imprint on our skin. But not all scars are visible. Some of the deepest wounds we carry are etched not on our bodies but on our hearts and souls.

As men, we often feel the pressure to hide these scars, to pretend they don't exist. We put on a brave face, we soldier on, we keep our pain hidden beneath a veneer of strength and stoicism. One of the ongoing themes in these reflections is to remind all of us that these unspoken hurts can shape our stories in profound ways, influencing our relationships, our self-image, and our sense of worth.

Some of these scars are self-inflicted, the result of our own poor choices and mistakes. We bear the marks of our own failings, our own sin. These are the scars we often feel the most shame about, the ones we try the hardest to conceal.

But many of our scars come from wounds that were inflicted on us. The harsh words of a parent, the betrayal of a friend, the trauma of abuse or neglect. These are the scars we carry through no fault of our own, the ones that can leave us feeling victimized, helpless, and alone.

Regardless of their origin, these scars can become a defining part of our story if we let them. They can keep us stuck in patterns of pain, bitterness, and fear. But that doesn't have to be the end of our story.

In Scripture, we see countless examples of people whose stories were marked by scars. People like **Joseph**, who bore the scars of betrayal and false accusation. Or **Paul**, who carried the physical scars of persecution and the emotional scars of his past as a persecutor of Christians. Yet in each of these stories, we see how God took these wounds and wove them into a greater narrative of redemption and hope.

Your scars are a part of your story, but they don't have to define it. **When you bring your scars to God, when you allow Him to touch your deepest wounds with His healing grace, He can use your pain to cultivate compassion, your brokenness to create a bridge to others who are hurting.**

This is a daily choice. That's one reason it's helpful to spend time daily pausing and reflecting on what's going on in your heart and your ongoing walk with Jesus. It's a decision to keep showing up, to keep bringing your scars into the light of God's love. It's a commitment to letting your wounds become windows for God's grace to shine through.

In the Japanese art of kintsugi, broken pottery is repaired with gold, silver, or platinum lacquer. The philosophy behind this is that the piece is more beautiful for having been broken. In the same way, as we allow God to heal our brokenness, our scars can become a testament to His redemptive power at work in our lives.

Don't hide your scars, but don't let them write the rest of your story either. Bring them to the Healer. Let Him bind up your wounds. Invite Him to transform your pain into a powerful story of grace, hope, and resilience.

REFLECTION: What scars—visible or invisible—do you continue carrying around with you? How do they continue shaping your story?

THE FREEDOM OF FORGIVENESS

As you're living out your story, carrying the wounds inflicted by others, it's easy to feel weighed down by anger and resentment. Each new hurt, no matter how small, adds to the burden you carry. Over time, this load can become heavy and cumbersome, hindering your ability to move forward and embrace the life God has for you.

Even when the load is heavy and we're feeling the weight caused by someone else, there are powerful reasons for us to forgive them. The most obvious reason is Scripture calls us to forgive each other as the Lord has forgiven us (Colossians 3:13). But also, even though it's not always easy, forgiving others is essential for your own healing and freedom.

As you take a step toward forgiving someone, it's important to understand what forgiveness is and isn't. **Forgiveness does not mean absolving someone of their guilt or responsibility, nor does it necessarily mean reconciling the relationship.** In cases of abuse or severe harm, reconciliation may not be wise or possible. **Rather, forgiveness is about releasing the hold that the offense and the offender have on your life.** It's about choosing to let go of the anger and pain, not always only for their sake but also for your own.

When you harbor unforgiveness, you remain emotionally tethered to those who have hurt you. Even if you never see them again, they maintain a level of control over your thoughts, feelings, and reactions. Forgiveness, on the other hand, is a declaration of your freedom. It's a way of saying, "What you did to me matters, but it no longer defines me. I choose to release you and the pain you've caused so that I can move forward into the life God has for me."

This process of forgiveness is not about minimizing or denying the reality of what you've suffered. It's about recognizing that holding on to the hurt only continues to harm you. Jesus tells us in Matthew 6:14–15, "if you forgive others their trespasses, your heavenly Father will also forgive you, but if you do not forgive others their trespasses, neither will your Father forgive your trespasses." **Forgiveness is a reflection of the grace we ourselves have received from God.**

As you consider extending forgiveness to those who have wounded you, remember the freedom and new life that await you on the other side. Imagine the lightness and peace you'll experience as you release the burdens you've carried for so long. Trust that as you step into this process, God will meet you with His strength, comfort, and healing.

REFLECTION: Take a moment to prayerfully consider any individuals you may need to forgive. Dad? Mom? Others? What anger, pain, or resentment have you been carrying with you? How might releasing these burdens through forgiveness bring new freedom and lightness to your life? Ask God to give you the courage and grace to extend forgiveness, not in your own strength, but in the power of His Spirit at work within you.

LIFTING THE MANHOLE COVER

Many of us have learned along the way to keep our feelings and emotions stowed deep inside ourselves, hidden away from the world. We cover them up with a heavy, guarded "manhole cover," designed to keep them out of sight and out of mind. But just like the complex systems beneath a city street, our emotional health needs regular maintenance and repair.

Lifting that manhole cover and peering inside our souls can feel daunting. Hopefully, this book of reflections is helping you do that on a daily basis. It's easy to fear what we might find lurking in the darkness—the pain, the wounds, the broken connections. But the truth is, we can't experience true healing and growth until we're willing to face what's inside.

When we take the brave step of removing our manhole cover and examining our inner world, we give ourselves the opportunity to see things as they really are. We can identify the faulty systems that are short-circuiting our lives, the roots of our reactions and behaviors. We can begin to make repairs, to rewire our thoughts and emotions in healthier ways.

God wants to meet us in the depths of our souls, in the places where we need Him most. David's prayer in Psalm 139:23–24 invites God to search and know his heart and to lead him. For those of us following Jesus, it's important to invite Him into those hidden

107

places on a daily basis and remind ourselves from His Word who He created us to be. His unending love and undeserved grace, when we truly receive them, can help transform us from the inside out.

This process of self-discovery and spiritual growth is a lifelong journey. It's an ongoing process. It takes daily reflection and requires us to consistently lift that manhole cover, allowing God to show us what's inside, and surrendering it all to Him. 2 Corinthians 5:17 promises that if you're in Christ, you're a new creation. The old is gone.

So, be courageous. **Lift that manhole cover and invite Jesus into the depths of your soul.** Allow God to show you the truth about yourself every new day—the good, the bad, and the broken. Receive the grace and love He so freely offers. It's a crucial step in becoming the man God created you to be.

> **REFLECTION:** Take some time to reflect on what might be lurking beneath your manhole cover today. What parts of your soul have you been hesitant to acknowledge or surrender to God? Ask Him to search your heart and reveal anything that needs His healing touch. Then, take a step of faith and invite Jesus into those places, trusting in His transformative power.

NAVIGATING THE JOURNEY WITH OTHERS

If you grew up without a father who provided guidance, affirmation, and a model of authentic manhood for you, then you more than likely have had occasions or seasons in your life when you've felt adrift, unsure of your identity and even uncertain about your path in life. Without a clear sense of direction, you may have struggled to navigate relationships, career, and personal growth.

It's never too late to find the mentorship and community that can help you chart your course toward authentic manhood. Scripture is filled with examples of the transformative power of mentorship. In 1 Kings 19, we see the prophet **Elijah** taking Elisha under his wing, preparing him to carry on his prophetic ministry. In the New Testament, **Paul** mentors Timothy, offering guidance and encouragement as the young man grows in his faith and leadership.

These biblical examples highlight the importance of seeking out men who are further along in their journey, men who embody the qualities and values of authentic manhood. By spending time with these mentors, by learning from their experiences and insights, you can begin to develop a clearer sense of your own identity and purpose.

But mentorship is not the only key to navigating the journey. **Equally important is the presence of a supportive community of peers—men who are also striving to live out authentic manhood alongside you.** Proverbs 27:17 reminds us that iron sharpens iron.

When men come together in genuine friendship and mutual encouragement, they spur one another on toward growth and maturity.

This kind of authentic community is modeled in the early church, where believers devoted themselves to fellowship, to breaking bread together, and to building each other up in love (Acts 2:42-47). When men engage in this type of **life-giving friendship**, they find the support, accountability, and joy that comes from walking the path together.

So if you find yourself feeling lost or alone in your journey toward authentic manhood, take heart. Seek out mentors who can offer wisdom and guidance. Surround yourself with a community of men who will encourage you, challenge you, and share in the ups and downs of life. "Two are better than one" (Ecclesiastes 4:9).

REFLECTION: Is there a man in your life whom you admire and respect, someone who could serve as a mentor to you? Consider reaching out to him, sharing your desire to learn and grow. Also, think about the friendships in your life. Are there men with whom you can build a community of mutual support and encouragement? Be sure you are investing in these relationships, knowing that navigating the journey together is always better than attempting to do it by yourself.

UNHEALTHY SHAME HINDERS HEALING

Shame can be a formidable barrier on our path to healing and authentic manhood. It whispers lies about our unworthiness, making us believe we're beyond the reach of God's love and grace. Ironically, it's precisely our unworthiness that makes His love and grace so remarkable. They are, by definition, undeserved gifts.

Brené Brown, a renowned researcher on shame, aptly notes, **"We all have it, we're all afraid to talk about it, and the less we talk about it, the more control it has over our lives** . . . shame is basically the fear of being unlovable."[1] This fear often intertwines with our wounds, creating a complex web of emotions.

We naturally yearn to be proud of our parents and to believe in the goodness of our own hearts. When reality falls short of these desires, shame can take root. Our wounds feed into our shame, and in turn, shame can prevent us from acknowledging, addressing, or healing from these wounds.

The key to breaking this cycle lies in bringing our shame into the light. By naming and discussing our shame, we begin to loosen its grip on our lives. This act of vulnerability not only initiates our healing process but also opens us up to receive the love and grace Jesus freely offers.

---

1. Brown, Brené. *The Gifts of Imperfection: Let Go of Who You Think You're Supposed to Be and Embrace Who You Are*. Simon and Schuster, 2022.

Remember, the love of Jesus has the power to shatter our shame. For those who follow Him, His love is unconditional. Ephesians 1:5–6 reminds us that He adopts us as His own children. This profound truth can revolutionize our perspective on shame.

Don't let shame hinder your journey toward healing and authentic manhood. Engage in honest conversations about your shame—with trusted friends, with God, with a counselor if needed. As you turn your shame over to Him, you'll find the freedom to confront your wounds and embrace the healing process.

REFLECTION: How is shame holding you back from owning your story and healing from your wounds? What specific areas of shame do you need to bring into the open?

BREAKING THE GENERATIONAL CYCLE OF PAIN

In families in which wounds go unhealed and pain goes unresolved, a destructive vortex can form. Like a hurricane or tornado, this vortex can sweep up everyone in its path, pulling them into a maelstrom of hurt and dysfunction. And the worst part? **This cycle doesn't stop with one generation. The pain is passed down, from parent to child, perpetuating a legacy of brokenness.**

This is the generational nature of unhealed wounds. We see it in the stories of our own families and in the pages of Scripture. Consider the family of **David.** His sin with Bathsheba and the murder of her husband set in motion a cycle of sexual sin, violence, and betrayal that played out in the lives of his children and grandchildren.

But the good news is that this cycle can be broken. The destructive inheritance of pain can stop with you. By God's grace, you can be the one who says, **"Enough. This ends with me."**

It takes courage. It takes authenticity. It means being willing to confront the wounds you carry, to bring them into the light of God's love. It means rejecting passivity and accepting the responsibility to seek healing, not just for yourself but for the sake of your family.

Accept responsibility for your own healing. The cycle of sin and pain can be broken by a generation that chooses to live differently.

This is where authenticity is so crucial. In order to break the cycle, you need to create an environment in your family where it's safe to be real, to talk about the hard things, the painful things. Where your spouse and children feel the freedom to share their fears, their hurts, their struggles.

No family has it all together, and pretending otherwise only perpetuates the cycle of hidden pain. But when you lead with vulnerability, when you invite your loved ones into the messy, unhealed parts of your story, you create space for healing to happen. You open the door for God's grace to come in and redeem what's been broken.

This is the heart of the gospel. That no matter how deep the wounds, no matter how long the cycle of pain has continued, God's love is deeper still. His power to heal and restore is greater than any generational curse.

So if you find yourself caught in the vortex of generational pain, know that you are not alone. Know that there is hope. And know that God is inviting you to be the change, to be the one who breaks the cycle.

It won't be easy. It will require you to lean into God's strength daily, to keep bringing your wounds and your family's wounds to the foot of the cross. But as you do, as you allow God's healing to flow into the broken places, you'll begin to see a new legacy take shape. A legacy of wholeness, of restoration, of grace.

REFLECTION: Consider the cycles of pain or dysfunction that may be present in your family history. How have these cycles affected you and your loved ones? What does it look like for you to break these cycles?

MOVING FORWARD IN GRIEVING AND GRACE

One crucial step in this healing journey is allowing yourself to grieve. It's tempting to want to rush past the pain, to push aside the sadness and the loss in an effort to move on. **But true healing requires acknowledging the hurt, giving yourself permission to feel it fully.** Ecclesiastes 3:4 reminds us that there is "a time to weep and a time to laugh, a time to mourn and a time to dance" (NIV). **Grieving is not a sign of weakness but of courage. It's a way of honoring your story and the impact it has had on you.**

As you grieve, remember to extend grace to yourself. You are not defined by your wounds or your mistakes. In Christ, you are a new creation (2 Corinthians 5:17). Embrace the grace that Jesus freely offers, allowing it to soften your heart toward yourself and others. This same grace can empower you to forgive those who have hurt you, not excusing their actions but releasing the hold they have on your life.

Healing is a process of learning and growth. As you reflect on your experiences, look for the lessons they hold. Perhaps you're gaining a clearer understanding of your own strength and resilience. Maybe you're learning to set healthier boundaries or to communicate your needs more effectively. **Trust that God can use even the most painful parts of your story to shape you into the man He's called you to be.**

There may be times when you feel like you're starting over, like you're learning to ride a bike again after a fall. But remember, you're not alone. God is with you, offering His strength and guidance every step of the way. Jeremiah 29:11 gives us a glimpse of the heart of God toward His people: "For I know the plans I have for you, declares the LORD, plans for welfare and not for evil, to give you a future and a hope."

As you continue on this journey of healing, hold fast to the hope you have in Christ. He is the Great Physician, the One who can bring wholeness and restoration to even the most broken places. Trust in His love for you and keep pressing forward in His grace.

> **REFLECTION:** Take a moment to bring your grief before the Lord. What do you need to acknowledge and release? Ask God to give you the courage to face your hurts and the grace to forgive. Consider the lessons and growth that may be emerging from your experiences. How might God be using your story to shape you and prepare you for the future He has for you?

Day Forty-Nine
FACING THE MONSTERS WITHIN

We all have monsters lurking in the shadows of our lives. The painful memories, the childhood traumas, the deep-seated fears that we try to ignore or suppress. **And these monsters don't just disappear when we close our eyes.** They continue to influence our thoughts, our choices, and our relationships, often in ways we're not even aware of.

They become the voices that whisper, "You're not good enough," "You'll never amount to anything," "You're unlovable."

You don't have to let these monsters control your story. **You have the power, through Christ, to face them head-on and to break their hold on your life**.

Scripture tells that we are from God and that He who is in us is greater than these monsters of fear, deception, and darkness (1 John 4:4). **The Spirit of God within you is mightier than any monster you face, more powerful than any of the negative whispers lurking in your mind.**

When you face your monsters with the light of God's love, you'll often find that they're not as powerful as you once believed. You'll see that the traumatic events of your childhood, while painful, do not define you. You'll discover that the negative beliefs you've held about yourself are distortions, not truths.

You have the ability to reframe your story, to see it through the lens of grace and redemption. And most importantly, you have the presence of a God who is bigger than any monster you face.

> **REFLECTION:** Take a moment to consider the "monsters" that may be lurking in your own story. What painful memories or experiences continue to influence you today? Remember, the light of His love can dispel even the darkest of shadows.

THE SHAPING POWER OF A FATHER'S WORDS

Words hold immense power, especially when they come from your dad. They can either build up or tear down, encourage or discourage, affirm, or critique. Proverbs 18:21 tells us that "death and life are in the power of the tongue." **The words spoken to you by your father have the power to shape your identity, your confidence, and your future.**

If you've grown up with a dad who affirmed you, expressed pride in you, and offered you physical affection and emotional availability, you've been gifted with a foundation of security and self-assurance. **Supportive dads engage in meaningful conversations with their sons, sharing their own struggles and triumphs, imparting wisdom gained from life's ups and downs.** They model humility by apologizing when they're wrong and demonstrating respect by listening to their sons' needs and dreams. Even in disagreement, they affirm their sons' growing identity and encourage healthy risk-taking. While no father is perfect, these dads understand the power of presence and affirmation.

The impact of having a healthy dad is often seen when these sons become dads themselves. They naturally tend to emulate the support and affirmation they received, passing on a legacy of love and encouragement to the next generation. Hence, the wisdom of Proverbs 22:6: "Train up a child in the way he should go; even when he is old he will not depart from it." The positive words and example of a father can guide a son in his own parenting journey.

Unfortunately, not all men have experienced this kind of fatherhood. Many have grown up with fathers who were absent, critical, emotionally disengaged, or even abusive. For these men, learning to be the affirming father they never had can be a challenge. If you lack a positive model to draw from, you may be struggling to find the right words and actions to connect with your own kids.

If you find yourself struggling to connect with your own kids, intentionality becomes key. By consciously choosing to speak words of affirmation, to share your own struggles and growth, and to prioritize emotional availability, **you can begin to break any negative cycles and establish a new legacy.** In Ephesians 4:29 we're encouraged to use our words to build others up and to benefit the ones we're speaking to. **Even in the midst of imperfection and ongoing growth, your authentic love and encouraging words can make a world of difference to your own kids.**

> **REFLECTION:** Reflect on your relationship with your dad and how it has influenced your own parenting or other relationships. Consider practical ways you can incorporate more affirmation and emotional availability into your interactions with your kids or others in your life. Your words and your presence have the power to shape lives and futures.

PAUSE AND REFLECT

Take a simple moment to pause today. Reflect on what's truly going on in your heart.

It's tempting to just keep going—pushing through life so you don't fall behind or miss out.

Stop. Reset your mind and your soul. Give yourself some time.

Give yourself some time with Jesus. Abide in Him. He says if you abide in Him, "you will know the truth, and the truth will set you free" (John 8:32).

Receive what Christ has for you today. He says that in Him, you can find pasture (John 10:9). In Him, you can find the spiritual food that will nourish your soul.

If you're in Christ, you are a new creation (2 Corinthians 5:17). You are made new in Him.

REFLECTION: Receive what Christ has for you today with open hands and an open heart.

THE COURAGE TO LEAN IN

There's a profound loneliness that can settle into our souls when we've been wounded by life. It's a feeling of being unworthy, unlovable, and, ultimately, alone. We build walls around our hearts, convinced that if people really knew us—our mistakes, our insecurities, our deepest fears—they would reject us. **So we resign ourselves to isolation, believing it's the only way to protect ourselves from further pain.**

We were never meant to live this life alone. From the very beginning, God designed us for relationship. He makes that clear in the creation story. We were created to connect, to love and be loved, to know and be known.

When we find ourselves trapped in the **"all-alone wound,"** healing begins with a courageous step: leaning in. **It's a daily choice to lean into God's love, to lean into honest self-reflection, and to lean into authentic relationships with others.**

Leaning into God's love requires faith. Even thinking about leaning fully into God's love may make you feel like the prodigal son in Luke 15, sheepishly returning home, unsure if you'll be welcomed or rejected because of your behavior or your doubts or your unworthiness. But just as the father in that story runs to embrace his son, our Heavenly Father is always ready to welcome you with open arms. His love is not based on your worthiness but on His grace.

Leaning into relationships with others requires vulnerability. It means gradually opening up to trusted friends, sharing your stories, your struggles, and your dreams. It means being honest about your need for support and connection. You may initially feel shaky or exposed. But as you're met with compassion and acceptance, you'll find yourself growing stronger, more rooted in your true identity.

The apostle Paul knew the power of leaning in. In Galatians 6:2, he writes, "Bear one another's burdens, and so fulfill the law of Christ." When we lean on each other, when we allow ourselves to be supported and loved in our struggles, we experience a taste of God's kingdom here on earth.

Of course, leaning in doesn't mean we'll never face rejection or hurt. People will let you down, because people are human. **But as we anchor our worth in God's unshakable love, we find the courage to keep showing up, keep reaching out, keep believing in the goodness of connection.**

So today, if you find yourself retreating into the shadows of isolation, take a deep breath and lean in. **Lean into the grace that is yours in Christ Jesus. Lean into the truth that you are loved by Him. Lean into the relationships that remind you you're never alone.** It's in this leaning that we find healing, wholeness, and the courage to live authentically.

> **REFLECTION:** In what ways have you found yourself pulling away from others, convinced you're unworthy of connection? What would it look like for you to lean in today—to God, to yourself, to a trusted friend? Remember, baby steps are still steps. Celebrate each courageous lean, knowing that you're moving toward the abundant life God has for you.

THE HEART WOUND

It's not exactly a newsflash to tell you we live in a broken world. But sometimes we forget just how deep that brokenness goes. We look around at all the pain, all the suffering, all the things that just don't seem right, and we wonder, "What's going on here?"

Scripture tells us that **this brokenness isn't just "out there." It's "in here," too. In our own hearts**. The apostle Paul knew this reality all too well in the midst of his own personal struggles. In Romans 7, he gets real about it. He says, "For I do not do the good I want, but the evil I do not want is what I keep on doing" (v. 19). Can you relate? I know I can.

Because of what happened way back in the Garden with Adam, our hearts got messed up. We all have a **"heart wound."** It's this inward bent, this tendency we all have to turn away from God and His good plan for us.

Some people might tell you that deep down, humans are naturally good. But that's not what Scripture teaches. It tells us that **our nature is bent, and it's bent away from God.** That's why it's so much easier to lose our cool than to keep it. It's why we find ourselves reacting in excessive anger or extreme selfishness, even when we know better.

Now, this doesn't mean we're as bad as we could be. There are plenty of things in place to restrain our worst impulses - things like laws, social expectations, our own conscience. But at the end of the day, no matter how "good" we might look compared to the next guy, we all fall short of God's standard. That's the bad news.

But here's the good news: **God didn't leave us stuck in this heart wound**. He didn't just tell us to try harder, to pull ourselves up by our moral bootstraps. No, He did something so much better. He sent Jesus.

While we were still a mess, while we were still stuck in our sin, Christ died for us (Romans 5:8). He took the punishment we deserved. He offered us forgiveness and a restored relationship with God, not based on what we can do for Him, but based on what He's done for us.

That's the only real solution to the original heart wound. Not self-help, not trying to be a better person, but putting our trust in Jesus. Letting Him heal us from the inside out.

So where does that leave us? Well, it means that as we walk this journey of authentic manhood, we don't have to pretend we've got it all together. We can be honest about our struggles, our failures, our need for grace. But it also means we don't have to stay stuck. **In Christ, we have the power to start living differently. To start living in the freedom and fullness He came to give us.**

It's a process, for sure. We're all works in progress. But as we keep turning to Jesus, as we keep letting Him shape and mold our hearts, we'll find ourselves becoming more and more the men He created us to be.

REFLECTION: Where are you feeling the effects of the heart wound in your life? What struggles, what sins, what tendencies are you wrestling with? Take a moment to thank God that you don't have to stay stuck. Thank Him for the gift of Jesus and the healing He offers. And ask Him to continue the work He's begun in you, shaping your heart to look more like His.

Day Fifty-Four

NOURISHING YOUR EMOTIONAL AND SPIRITUAL HEALTH

Just as our physical body needs regular hydration to function at its best, our soul needs consistent nourishment to thrive. But in the midst of packed schedules, pressing responsibilities, and the weight of unaddressed wounds, it's all too common to push this essential self-care to the back burner.

Proverbs 4:23 reminds us to "keep your heart with all vigilance, for from it flow the springs of life." **Your emotional and spiritual health is the wellspring from which all other areas of your life are affected.** When you take the time to attend to your inner world, to connect with God, yourself, and others in meaningful ways on a daily basis, you replenish your reserves and find the strength to navigate life's challenges.

Neglecting this vital nourishment can leave you feeling depleted, anxious, and disconnected. You may find yourself struggling to engage fully in your work, your relationships, and your personal growth. It's in these moments that the gentle reminder to prioritize your emotional and spiritual health is most needed.

I believe the most powerful way to nourish your soul is by leaning into the love and grace of Jesus. He invites those of us who are laboring and are heavy laden to come to Him, and He promises

127

to give us rest (Matthew 11:28). When you bring your burdens, your wounds, and your weariness to the feet of Jesus, He meets you with compassion, understanding, and the strength to keep going.

Cultivating emotional and spiritual health also involves fostering deep, authentic connections with others. I know, I know. That's a repeated theme throughout these reflections. It feels redundant. And it is redundant because it's so important for us to be reminded we were created for community, for the kind of relationships that allow us to be seen, known, and supported. And too many guys go through life just living on the surface and missing out on all of the blessings, encouragement, growth, and freedom that comes from deep, authentic community. Don't let that be you. Make it a priority to nourish your emotional and spiritual health.

> **REFLECTION:** Where do you feel depleted or disconnected in your life? What practices or relationships help you feel most nourished and replenished? Invest in your emotional and spiritual well-being by setting aside time daily to pray, to be with Jesus, to meditate in Scripture. Tending to your soul is not a luxury but a necessity.

THE RIVER WITHIN

Deep within each of us lies an untouched, unrefined cavern of memories, experiences, emotions, and images. **I like to picture within that cavern a flowing river—a pure, underground spring that holds the key to authentic manhood.**

This river is the love and presence of Jesus in your soul. It's the living water that Jesus spoke of in John 4:14. He said, "Whoever drinks of the water that I will give him will never be thirsty again. The water that I will I give him will become in him a spring of water welling up to eternal life." This river runs through you, empowering you, guiding you, and fueling you with His love and grace.

It's important to acknowledge the rocks and obstacles that have hindered the river's flow. These are the wounds, the fears, the doubts that you've clung to, the stalagmites and stalactites of your inner cavern. Sometimes you've clung to them in ways that have kept you from fully enjoying the river. They've shaped you, yes, but they don't have to define you.

The journey to authentic manhood includes learning to let go of these rocks and step into the river of Jesus's love. It's a process of detaching from your past, not by ignoring or defying it but by meeting it head-on, greeting it with compassion, and then releasing it into the rush of grace.

As you immerse yourself in this river, you'll find a new kind of freedom. The rapids of life will still come, but you'll navigate them with a sense of purpose, identity, and security that can only be found in Christ. As Romans 8:37–39 declares, "No, in all these things we are more than conquerors through him who loved us. For I am sure that neither death nor life, nor angels nor rulers, nor present things nor things to come, nor powers, nor height nor depth, nor anything else in all creation, will be able to separate us from the love of God in Christ Jesus our Lord."

So dare to step into your internal river. **Let the love and presence of Jesus rush over you, refreshing you, nourishing you, and propelling you into the rest of your story.** It's not about the scenery of your past or the landscape of your future. It's about the exhilaration of riding the rapids hand-in-hand with your Savior.

> **REFLECTION:** Has life felt difficult, weighty, or hard? Do you sometimes see your journey more as a desert of thorns than a white-water adventure with Jesus? Ask Jesus to show you the river of His love that flows within you. Pray for the courage to let go of the rocks you've been clinging to and step into the rush of His grace.

INTENTIONAL TIME, INTENTIONAL TALK

For you guys who are dads, obviously, spending time with your kids is invaluable. But it's important to remember the *quality* of that time is just as important as the **quantity. As a dad, you have the unique opportunity to shape your kids' hearts,** to impart wisdom, and to create a lifelong bond that goes beyond surface-level interactions. If you're not a dad, allow these words to help you reflect on the quality of your connection with your own dad.

Scripture is filled with examples of dads who took the time to have meaningful conversations with their children. In Deuteronomy 6:6–7 **Moses** instructs the Israelites, "These commandments that I give you today are to be on your hearts. Impress them on your children. Talk about them when you sit at home and when you walk along the road, when you lie down and when you get up" (NIV). This passage emphasizes the importance of intentionally sharing spiritual truths and life lessons with your children in the context of daily life.

When you spend time with your kids, make it a point to delve into the real stuff—the deep questions, the heart matters, the spiritual wrestling. Talk about faith, relationships, character, and purpose. Share your own struggles and triumphs, your hopes and fears. By opening up in this way, you create a safe space for your kids to do the same, fostering a connection that will endure through the years.

If your own dad modeled this kind of intentional, heart-level engagement, this may come easy for you. But even if you didn't have that example, it's never too late to start. Seek out other dads who are doing this well and learn from their approach. Pray for wisdom and guidance as you navigate these meaningful conversations with your kids.

This isn't to say that every moment together needs to be heavy or serious. There's immense value in the light-hearted, fun times you spend together—the laughter, the play, the shared adventures. But don't let those moments crowd out the intentional conversations that will shape their character and your relationship.

The apostle Paul's relationship with Timothy is a beautiful example of a spiritual father investing deeply in his son in the faith. In 2 Timothy 3:14–15 Paul reminds Timothy, "But as for you, continue in what you have learned and have become convinced of, because you know those from whom you learned it, and how from infancy you have known the Holy Scriptures, which are able to make you wise for salvation through faith in Christ Jesus" (NIV). Paul's intentional teaching and modeling left an indelible mark on Timothy's life and faith.

As a dad, you have the same opportunity to leave a lasting impact on your kids. But time slips by quickly, and before you know it, they will be grown and on their own. Don't let those precious years pass without being intentional about the deeper things you want to impart.

REFLECTION: Set aside some time this week for a meaningful conversation with your kids. Come prepared with a few questions or topics you want to discuss, but also be open to where the conversation leads. Maybe share a struggle you've been facing and what you're learning through it, or ask your kids about their own challenges and dreams. Pray together, affirming your love and God's love for them. Make this kind of intentional, heart-level time a regular part of your relationship, and watch the bond between you grow deeper and stronger.

Day Fifty-Seven

FROM OBSERVER TO PARTICIPANT

You may find yourself struggling to navigate the process of change. **It's not uncommon as a man to feel disconnected from your own heart, treating life and relationships as an objective observer rather than an engaged participant.** You might find safety in remaining detached, watching others and yourself from a distance.

This detachment can feel like a form of self-protection. By relying solely on reason and logic, you can avoid the messiness and vulnerability of emotions. You might assess situations and people, evaluating their actions at arm's length without fear of reciprocation. When you disconnect from your own heart, you risk missing out on the fullness of life and relationships that God intends for you.

Jesus models the importance of engaging with our emotions in a healthy way. In John 11:35, we see Him weeping at the tomb of Lazarus. We also see Him pouring out His heart to His Heavenly Father the night before his crucifixion. Our Savior, fully God and fully man, was not afraid to feel deeply and express his emotions. As men created in God's image, we are called to do the same.

Engaging with your emotions doesn't mean being controlled by them but rather learning to understand and steward them well. Psalm 139:23–24 invites us to pray, "Search me, O God, and know my heart! Try me and know my thoughts! And see if there be any grievous way in me, and lead me in the way everlasting." When you invite God into the process of exploring your inner world, He can bring light to the dark places and guide you toward healing.

And don't forget to invite trusted others to walk alongside you. James 5:16 encourages us to "confess your sins to one another and pray for one another, that you may be healed." **Who in your life can you trust to speak truth to you, to see things about you that you may not readily see?** This is a common theme in these reflections, but so many men go through life without this support. They miss out on truly seeing themselves as others see them and enjoying the freedom that comes from walking authentically with other men. Pray for discernment and courage as you open yourself up to this kind of support.

Remember, **the goal is not just self-awareness but also active engagement**. As you learn to connect with your own heart and invite others into your journey, you'll find yourself shifting from passive observer to active participant in your own life and relationships.

REFLECTION: Are there areas of your life where you tend to remain a detached observer? What fears or past hurts might be contributing to this detachment? Take a step toward vulnerability and active engagement this week, knowing that God is with you and for you in the process.

Day Fifty-Eight

STEPPING OUT FROM BEHIND THE SCREEN

In today's world, **we're more connected than ever**. Social media, instant messaging, video calls—technology has made it possible to interact with people across the globe at the touch of a button. And yet, **paradoxically, we're also lonelier than ever**. Behind our screens, we can curate an image, a persona that we present to the world. But too often, that persona is a facade behind a glass wall that keeps us from truly engaging with life and with others.

It's like standing before a breathtaking mountain range but only being able to view it through a window. We can appreciate its beauty, imagine what the crisp mountain air might feel like in our lungs, but we can't fully experience it. We're observers, not participants.

God didn't create us to live behind glass walls. He didn't design us for a life of isolation and spectatorship. Jesus came to invite us into the abundant life, a life of authenticity, of deep connection with Him and with others.

Breaking out from behind the screen, shattering that glass wall, can be scary. We've grown accustomed to the safety of our barriers, the control we have over what we reveal and what we conceal. But as long as we stay behind the glass, we're missing out on the richness of real, face-to-face relationships, heart-to-heart relationships, the joy of being fully known and fully loved.

The apostle Paul understood this. In 1 Thessalonians 2:8, he writes, "Because we loved you so much, **we were delighted to share with you**

135

not only the gospel of God but our lives as well" (NIV). Paul didn't just preach at people from behind a pulpit. He shared his life with them. He invited them into his struggles, his joys, his day-to-day existence.

That's the kind of authentic manhood God calls us to. Not a life of performance and pretense, but a life of vulnerability and connection. **It's a life where we're not afraid to admit our weaknesses, because we know that's where God's strength shines through (2 Corinthians 12:9).** It's a life where we're willing to take off our masks and let people see the real us, trusting that we'll be loved and accepted, flaws and all.

This saying has often been attributed to poet and philosopher Henry David Thoreau: **"Most men lead lives of quiet desperation and go to the grave with the song still in them."**

So how do we start? By taking small steps of courage. By initiating a lunch with a friend and daring to go beyond surface-level conversation. By joining a small group of men where we can be supported and challenged in our life and in our faith. By putting down our phones and giving our full attention to the people in front of us.

As we step out from behind our screens, as we shatter the glass that's been holding us back, we'll find a new freedom. We'll discover the joy of being part of a community, of laughing and crying and growing together. We'll experience the depth of love that comes from being genuinely seen and known.

So today take a step. Reach out. Risk being known. **Trust that as you shatter the glass and step into authentic manhood, God will meet you there with His grace, His strength, and His boundless love.**

REFLECTION: What glass walls have you been hiding behind? What holds you back from pursuing authentic relationships? Take a moment to pray for the courage to take a step toward vulnerability and connection today. Look around for the people He's placed in your life to support and encourage you along the way.

Day Fifty-Nine

OVERCOMING ANXIETY AND EMBRACING HEALING

It's easy to view our wounds as weaknesses, something to be hidden away and ignored. We fear that acknowledging our pain and struggles will somehow diminish us, making us less of a man in the eyes of others and ourselves. **But the danger in that is these unaddressed wounds can fuel a pervasive anxiety that affects every area of our lives, often in ways we're not even aware of.**

Proverbs 12:25 tells us, "Anxiety in a man's heart weighs him down, but a good word makes him glad." When we allow our wounds to fester, when we try to push through the pain on our own strength, we carry a heavy burden that can rob us of joy, purpose, and the abundant life God desires for us.

These anxieties can manifest in various ways. Perhaps you find yourself struggling to connect deeply with others, always holding a part of yourself back out of fear of rejection or judgment. Maybe you pour yourself into your work or other distractions, trying to outrun the discomfort that comes with stillness and introspection. Or perhaps you turn to unhealthy coping mechanisms, seeking temporary relief from the pain but ultimately compounding your struggles.

But there is hope. "The LORD is near to the brokenhearted and saves the crushed in spirit" (Psalms 34:18). When you bring your wounds and anxieties to God, when you invite Him into the painful places of your story, He meets you with compassion, understanding, and the power to heal.

As you engage in this process, you'll find that the anxieties that once held you back begin to lose their grip. You'll discover a newfound freedom to embrace your God-given gifts, to pursue your passions, and to live out your purpose with renewed energy and vitality.

Your wounds do not have to define you. They are part of your story, but in Christ you are a new creation (2 Corinthians 5:17), deeply loved and cherished by your Heavenly Father. As you lean into His love and grace, as you embrace the healing He offers, you'll find yourself more empowered to live out the purposeful and abundant life He has for you.

> **REFLECTION:** Take a moment to prayerfully consider any anxieties that may be holding you back from living fully into your God-given purposes. What fears or past hurts do you need to bring into the light of God's love? Set aside dedicated time for prayer and reflection, and share your anxieties with the Lord.

Day Sixty

EMBRACING THE JOURNEY

We've been on quite a journey together. Fittingly, we're closing out this journey to better understand our own story by talking again about **the one wound we all share: the heart wound—this inward bent we all have, this tendency to turn away from God and His good plan for us.** We've seen how it affects us, how it can lead us into some pretty dark places if we're not careful.

This is a great reminder for all of us—even after putting our faith in Jesus and committing to follow Him as our Savior, even when we've been forgiven, we're still in process. God's Spirit is at work in us, shaping our desires, aligning our hearts more and more with His. And we still wrestle with that old nature. We still have to contend with the lingering effects of the heart wound.

One of those effects, especially for us as men, is this tendency to rely on ourselves rather than God. We think we've got to have it all together, that we don't need anyone's help. So we put on a facade, and we hide what's really going on inside. We do the same thing Adam did when he sinned—we try to hide from God and from our own feelings.

That's a dangerous game. **When we disconnect from our heart, when we stuff down those emotions and experiences, it's like a ticking time bomb.** Sooner or later, they're going to come out—in anger, in addiction, in all sorts of destructive ways.

139

How do we counter this tendency to disconnect? Well, Chip Dodd, in his book *The Voice of the Heart*, gives us three suggestions.

First, we've got to get real with our feelings. We've got to take responsibility for what's going on in our hearts. That means not just acknowledging our emotions but actually feeling them—the hurt, the loneliness, the fear, all of it.

This doesn't mean we let our emotions run the show. It's not about indulging every feeling that comes along. But it's also not about stuffing them down and pretending they don't exist. It's about being honest with ourselves and with God.

This leads to the second suggestion: we've got to tell the truth about our hearts to people we trust. We've got to move beyond surface-level conversations and get real with each other. That's where true friendship happens, where we can find accountability and support.

Yes, opening up like that can be scary. We worry that people won't like what they see, that we're the only ones struggling. But the truth is, we're all in the same boat. Every temptation, every challenge you face, other men are facing it too.

Finally, and most importantly, we've got to bring the truth of our hearts to God. We've got to get honest with Him in prayer, sharing our joys, our frustrations, our failures, all of it. Look at the psalms—David didn't hold back. He laid it all out there before God.

And that's the invitation for us. To come to God just as we are, heart wound and all, and let Him meet us there.

This is the journey of authentic manhood. It's not about having it all together. It's about being honest about where we're at and continually turning to the One who can heal and transform us.

As we close out this series of reflections, I want to encourage you: keep going. Keep pressing into Jesus. Keep being honest with yourself, with others, and with God. **Keep setting aside time daily to** pause, ponder, and reflect on the deeper things in life. The things that matter most. It's a daily choice, a daily surrender.

We're all on this journey together, stumbling forward by grace. So let's keep spurring each other on, pointing each other to the truth, and watching as God does His transforming work in us.

REFLECTION: Where do you sense God calling you to even greater honesty and vulnerability? Remember, growth is a process. Celebrate each step forward, trusting that God is at work in you, shaping your heart to look more like His.

SCAN HERE to learn more about
Invite Ministries—created to invite people to a deeper
faith and living relationship with Jesus Christ